ALL THE LIVELONG DAY

Also by
RICHARD NEIL

Serenader

ALL THE LIVELONG DAY

THE THANKSGIVING WRECK AT WOODSTOCK

RICHARD NEIL

Arboretum Publishing Company USA

The epigraph is from a traditional nursery rhyme and song, "I've Been Working on the Railroad". "The Wabash Cannonball" is also traditional. "Invictus" by William Ernest Henley was written in the 19th century and recited from memory. "I Like to See It Lap the Miles", # 585, is too a 19th century poem from *The Poems of Emily Dickinson*, edited by Thomas H. Johnson, 1955, and included in *Major Writers of America II*, Harcourt, Brace & World, Inc., 1962.

Thanks to Bob Hasty, Amtrak Agent, Birmingham, Alabama, who knowingly and unknowingly sparked this account and allowed for its truthful nature. National Transportation Safety Board transcripts proved key. Thanks to my mother for title and Robert M. Gambrell, Jr. and Dean A. Gambrell, Sr. for knowledge and guidance. And a special thanks to railroaders.

This is a work of nonfiction, but observation and memory are indeed imperfect.

Library of Congress Control Number: 2023904078
Neil, Richard.
All the Livelong Day: the Thanksgiving wreck at Woodstock/Richard Neil

ISBN 978-0-9787772-1-0

Front cover and inside photographs from the original Gambrell Family Collection.
Cover design and back cover photos Richard Neil.

richardneil.net
richardneilworks@gmail.com

First Printing, 2024

For my parents

Contents
~~

~~

I've been working on the railroad
All the livelong day
I've been working on the railroad
Just to pass the time away
~~Traditional

1

Eddy Gulch

Each morning my job begins by climbing to an elevation of 6,400 feet or thereabout. For an aging frustrated forester who entered his field to live and work among America's western wildlands, little looks better than a panoramic view from a deserted mountain top knife edge. From so high, Salmon River drainage and watershed below appears a series of sharp "V" shaped canyons and gullies spreading westward, as rolling waves, from a rocky Southern Cascade Mountain Crest and Pacific Trail on east, several thousand feet above, to California's northwesternmost coast 100 miles or so away. Though only sometimes visible so deep below, a carved valley tributary—wet, dry, or intermittent—hides beneath each ridge line. If wet, it rushes fast, clear, and cold until it dumps into one of a half dozen or more slow, deep rivers near sea.

North from Eddy Gulch, several thousand feet higher on a plateau, a wilderness sprawls for scores of miles and, day and night, displays glowing white marble outcroppings throughout.

Southward, Trinity Alps, as their European namesake, impose cathedralic magnitude and magnificence upon everything and everyone in pastel hues and alpine glow. In highest country, mini glaciers in "U" shaped basins disappear and cease existence.

My initial purpose up top in tower consists of watching, looking, and waiting. Most who come up here have doubts about longevity. People last minutes, hours, days, weeks, months, a season, or years depending on will and ability to withstand solitude, boredom, weather, and sometimes fear of heights and altitude sickness. Regardless of duration, even hardiest visitors welcome return to solid ground. If up long enough, knees feel weak and soles airy when feet rejoin Mother Earth.

Eddy Gulch differs from most fire towers—serving as an historical outpost for a first female lookout in 1912 and a communication center relaying radio messages for Forest Service employees in desolate country, both unique.

Folks back east imagine fire towers as tiny boxlike cabs, 4x4 or 8x8. Western towers in California and elsewhere measure, with little exception, much larger, maybe 16x16 or 18x18 with convertible sofa/cot, comfortable office chairs, gas stove and heat, fridge, shower, hot water, sink, plumbing, fans, and occasionally air conditioning and TV. They feel like an office or efficiency apartment, a cool *pad* in sky.

A small number of outdoors enthusiasts, hikers, canoeists, cyclists, anglers come to Klamath National Forest, but descendants of early settlers and Hoopa Indians comprise most of a handful of isolationists one encounters on a long hot or cool, depending on elevation, day in paradise. Up in tower or down below, most days find few humans except in summer months when Pacific Trail walkers trek through and stayover in Etna to reload on supplies, eats, drinks, energy, and resolve.

From a fire tower, things look different. On a clear day, an eye strains to discern mist and fog along ocean edge, maybe a glimmer of salty water and air. You know an ocean lay out there and your mind says you see it or at least an aqua silvery glare. You know for sure you can make out frequent and quite famous Northwest Coast fog, but old timers and newcomers differ on whether Pacific water can be made out by a naked eye from as far away as Eddy Gulch, a 100-mile shot. For me, she's visible—there she blows. If you're up here long enough, you see most anything, ocean included, or think you do. You allow yourself to drift, indulge, but above all—it's a matter of perspective.

In fire season, most days come and go as ones before and after—sun, cool wind, sometimes a few clouds below, and almost non-existent rain and moisture. One old timer, human for over three-quarters century and fire lookout for over a decade, wishes you Happy Sailing as he comes and goes and whistles.

Incessant winds blow. Sunlight heats exposed mountain sides and tops faster than shady streams and riverbeds, significant pressure gradients build, and updrafts form up draws and bluffs. In evening, an opposite occurs, exposed tops lose heat first, warm air below rises, and cool air rushes down. Maritime eastward flow augments a constant state of atmospheric flux.

Some days a bear walks through camp just as inquisitive about a human inside tower and what he eats as vice versa. Deer come to a salt lick placed nearby by their Forest Service friends. Golden eagles soar, swoop, and glide on rising air, and vultures dine on abundant carrion. A large five-foot Northern Pacific Rattler, maybe 4 to 5 inches diameter, lives about 30 feet away from tower. He suns undetected among rocks on most days, blending with precise pigments of his bright orange, yellow, and corral colored home. A fat, bushy gray squirrel toys and teases him, and in response, he coils and rattles, but mostly ignores his old furry friend. They know each other—going way back.

Hawks hang around nearby and perch on limbs or rocks or sometimes on tower railing and wait too—like you—searching for movement. Their claws clasp and hold a motionless stance for what seems forever, until at long last a mouse or reptile or chipmunk or ground squirrel budges and avian predatory instinct screams, *There the som'bitch is. Right there.*

Young fire starts might be a wisp from behind a hill or ledge or a puff or raging stream or column of smoke or a campfire shaped plume coming from trees or most anywhere. Unlike many areas of California and elsewhere, Eddy Gulch and Salmon River maintain isolated solitude—little human activity. Most who venture in or out —depending on viewpoint—of Klamath forests possess outdoor experience and resulting fire savvy. Lightning causes almost all fires, humans a scarce few.

You wait and watch so long your eyes play tricks. You don't want to miss it. You don't want a plane or helicopter working a fire elsewhere to fly over and spot it and steal your thunder and make you feel ever so impotent and worthless. And you don't want some pain in ass using a cell phone to beat you. How embarrassing. Even more so, you don't want an undetected fire on your watch.

You sit and stand and wait some more and some more. You scan 360 degrees every ten minutes or so. You watch. You check out false indicators. No, not a fire—just vapor or reflection or glare or dust. You play fire's waiting game.

And then something begins to happen. You heard thunder, maybe last night and maybe a few minutes before. Thunderheads line in row. You hear thunder for sure this time. You look. Maybe some rain moistened a spark and some duff smolders underground and you can't see it. A blinding flash and simultaneous crash of lightning almost knock you off mountain. You look some more. Rain and haze moving in and obstruct your view. And when you feel unable to look anymore and wait anymore, there it is, some white appears. Maybe it's vapor—what's known in fire country as water dogs. Moisture gets caught under warm rock then releases in what looks something like smoke. You look closer with binoculars and lo and behold it appears to be streaming and has a heat induced inconsistency vapor doesn't have. Adrenaline pumps, and your ever-loving fire detecting, unrewarded, and always isolated mind screams, *There the som'bitch is. Right there.*

You want to detect smoke early. Size it up. Locate it on a contour map. Call it in with an azimuth reading and approximate distance and legal description. You convey to a dispatcher what you know instead of what you think. You figure a route to fire and assess any obstacles and unusual characteristics caused by wind, aspect, slope, vegetation, structure, human activity so you can pass them to first responders. In 10 or 15 minutes, most of your job ends barring a request for more information from firemen or air support or dispatcher. Look for a next one.

Last summer in a three-day period, 32 fires broke out around Eddy Gulch. Resources to attack fires became strained and overwhelmed. As always, preference belonged to fires nearer property and to ensuring human safety. Most fires received immediate attack and quick suppression, but five or six fires burned for hours and days before anyone attacked them. *Wildfire travels like bad news.* A few unattended fires exploded, burned together, spotted to form larger fires, and lasted months. Hundreds of thousands of acres scorched at almost unimaginable cost, effort, and manpower—over a thousand people working each day on one mega-blaze until a fire season ending event—autumn or winter—cool air, moisture, rain, snow, ice.

Fire fighters dislike working Salmon River country, its ruggedness almost insurmountable—one steep rocky ridge and ledge adjacent to another with few clearings and meadows for crews to work and station.

Some firemen, a certain breed or mold, do it well with dedication and deserve commendation. Sometimes they get it. Communities and local businesses put up bulletin boards expressing thanks and even list names of "heroes". Good deeds sometimes go noticed. But when smoke from fire hangs thick enough to essentially shut down an entire town, and fire camps grow so large with personnel and equipment as to look as if military in war, one wonders about mistakes, misdeeds, resources, and process. Visitors to a fire tower sometimes depart down metal steps looking back and bidding, Thank you for your service.

But on top, I think I see more, gain advantage, enhance perception. It carries over to life where I always take a room with a view, go a route with a vista, make my one-time ceiling my all-time floor. Better perception might magnify dreams and images, allow fulfillment of goals, aspirations, plans, and understanding.

At season's end, I drive southwest to Reno, rent an upper-level room and next day cruise toward Colorado and across summits and The Divide. From there, interstate leads me to country roads, and they take me a high road to Blue Ridge overlooks and Smoky Mountain passes and back through northern Alabama and Little River Canyon to Birmingham.

My apartment perches on Red Mountain, just below a cast iron statue of Vulcan—god of fire and metalworking—hundreds of feet above city, spear in hand, hammer at side. He overlooks city, he knows perspective. A lot of incorrigible cynics don't like him because he's half naked, generally speaking, but in his defense, his makers bear responsibility for his exposure, not he. Of all Romans America has witnessed, Vulcan holds enviable position, way up high like that—he sees all and allows others same. Afterall, church steeples reach toward heaven, to be higher, to glorify, to know and see all and be closer. Maybe from somewhere above, a story might be better perceived and constructed. Perhaps, up there, vision leads to reason and comprehension of human error below, playing out in obvious, predictable, and somehow avoidable ways.

Robert Burns wrote, in a translated paraphrase of his Scottish tongue, Best laid plans of mice and men often go astray. He plowed up a field mouse home disrupting a rodent's winter preparation and existence forever. He stood high above broken earth and ruined nest—seeing it better from above. He realized—poet he was—unintended action or error changes in a split second—for mice and men —what creates in days, weeks, months, years, decades, centuries, or ages.

From mountain pedestal, Vulcan views a mechanical city—a Magic City—hears rumbling rails, observes skyline, and imagines how a view differed decades ago, without a building here and a bridge there, minus a freeway system, before air conditioning, without this big sign and that bright light. He might see a forest at a distance and visualize it with or without fire, and he might look down on Jones Valley below and see trains and conceptualize train track paths today much as they existed long before. He hears train whistles. He might, just maybe, be able to know rampant mistakes in life below.

John Lennon sang of a fool on a hill who saw it all—a world spinning round, a sun going down, and disdain from people below.

Long ago, in University of Alabama Sociology 101, a wise professor had 10 people leave his room. He then chose one person to witness an action or incident. One by one he allowed those 10 people to reenter, and his Witness told Person One what happened in his absence. Person One told entering Person Two who told entering Person Three and so on until all people were back in room.

By Person 10, action or incident first observed became unrecognizable, completely different from actual occurrence. An auditorium of onlooking students roared hysterical laughter as "bad" accounts relayed person to person became more and more erroneous and sometimes bizarre.

When stories resurrect and characters and action recreate, legends alter, blemish, glorify. Early settlers to Redwoods of Northwest California caught lamprey, a jawless fish, but thought and called them eels and named their fishing hole Eel River, its name today. An exaggeration, mischaracterization, miscalculation, white lie changes a tale forever.

From up here high on Red Mountain, a railroader's story and hospital bed, miles and cities and decades away, feels close, touchable, and reachable—bright globe lights centering a barren hallway leading to a dim room, doctors and nurses in and out. Always strong, proud, and faithful, and fighting welling eyes, he told me, They say I may never walk again.

2

Never Speak Harsh Words

Good, sober railroad men awake early and arrive on time; in 1951, their women do too. Robert climbs out first, stands naked, and inspects his bedstead. Near his wife's head a loud, behind time self-winding alarm clock ticks across oak floor. Railroaders and military require precision. His fingers, powerful, capable, and always a little shaky, pull his Hamilton pocket watch from olive workpants he laid out night before—4:10.

Robert always sleeps light and gets up early when going out on a run. He flips Hamilton's lid closed. In his palm, he holds two inches diameter of gold—cool, smooth, heavy, resistant, impene-trable—unconquerable time.

From his bedroom window, he looks out through near darkness over five acres of, in those days, rural eastern greater Birmingham, a few miles away from a site to become, in a few years, Norris Yard, a new expansive freight yard. Near his new home,

Alabama Great Southern Railroad, part of the Southern Railway system, tracks run northeast toward Gadsden, Ft. Payne, Lookout Mountain, and Chattanooga. His white board, two-bedroom house measures maybe 60x30 with a flat tar and gravel roof and little outbuilding behind.

Robert tugs pants, tucks white tee, and barefoots to a red brick fireplace, rising to ceiling, and stokes it as he once fired steam locomotives. Dim Willow Lane streetlight through Venetian blinds allows him a sketchy evaluation of his new living room. He figures, when he returns from Meridian tomorrow, he and Buster, his carpenter friend neighbor, will resume a monstrous task of do-it-yourself home building, now nearing completion. Buster provides craftsmanship, and Robert scrapes up money and assists best he can. Most, Buster included, consider Mr.-Fix-It least fitting of Robert's many identities.

Firelight grows. Robert revisits his watch—4:24. *Three hundred and fifty-one miles to his southwest, a switching engine moves a tavern-lounge-observation car onto Track #2 of New Orleans Terminal, a station appearing more monumental than functional, built on "neutral ground", local for median, at Rue Bassin and Canal Street in French Quarter. Most railroads shared passenger facilities throughout Southeast, but the Southern Railway often, as in Birmingham and New Orleans, preferred its own. It separates them from the rest, elevates them in a region essential for existence and predominance. Their station looks elongated, marbled, picturesque, stately or majestic, and white.*

This tail car, alone on Track 2, becomes a seed of The Southerner northbound, Train #48, a 7 A.M. departure for New York City and all stops in between.

Understand, a railroad man relies on his precious pocket watch. He hesitates and dawdles little, and like a military man most were those days, he gets more done before 9 AM than most do all day. He sticks to a plan—his work order, he avoids taking anything for granted, he shuns error, and he repudiates daydreaming until doomsday.

By habit, he slides his timepiece into a small slit watch pocket above right front hip pocket, feels to assure its 12-inch gold braided chain wraps around belt loop and T-bar fob rests in pocket —designed and done to order as railroad and military do. He hits shower, boy.

Geraldine moves next, sits up, tries to make out her alarm clock's status, and goes straight to her beveled mirror, surrounded by swirls of arcs and loops, sitting atop her mama's antique chest of drawers. So early, she wishes mirrors lied as alarm clocks do.

Gerry, as friends call her, pulls back her hair, but finds it difficult to manage and a ponytail too much an undertaking. She shakes her head, lets her strands fall, and mutters something akin to, Oh, Geraldine. As Gerry often does when using her formal given name, she utters, Poor Mama, speaking of her adoptive mother who she considers angel on earth.

Robert rising seldom plays in silence, and Gerry hears loud and clear. Shower sounds fill their home, light under a lone bathroom door radiates. He's singing something about whether Juicy Fruity gum loses flavor on a bedpost overnight. She shrugs and shakes her head.

Gerry's parents adopted her in 1923, shortly after birth. She knew them as her only parents, she wanted only them, and she lacked reason to look for others. She considered her adopted parents Mama and Daddy; she cherished them, and they her. Their oldest biological son, Gerry's brother by her adoption, died after being run over by a car two blocks from their home on First Avenue in front of Woodlawn High School in 1926.

Gerry and Robert married in early 1942. She worked as a secretary-administrative assistant while Robert took a job at Conners Steel, a manufacturing plant by railroad tracks in Woodlawn, almost four miles east of downtown Birmingham. He had completed two years at Howard College, later Samford University, using his steel worker earnings to pay his way. Woodlawn dates to early 19th Century plantation presence before Birmingham existed.

World War II caused Robert to enlist as a marine a few months after marriage. Following Parris Island training, railroads took him across country to California and ships carried him west to South Pacific destinations, a long way from rural Alabama beginnings.

At war's end, Robert came home to Birmingham, his wife, son, and steel mill. In 1946, he went to work shoveling coal as a fireman on the Southern Railway. In a few years, diesel engines evolve, steam locomotives disappear as if dinosaurs, and life becomes easier as it did for many who feed fires of trains and heavy industry in a modernizing, booming post-war South.

Gerry *junes* to kitchen and pushes up a light switch causing four 6-foot-long fluorescent tube bulbs to crackle and, after several false starts, glow. She puts on a 10-inch-tall aluminum Comet coffee pot with molded brown rubber handles and thimble-sized percolation bubble centered on top. She places it on a back burner of a new, glistening white enamel GE range and stove with single door, flush corners, and flat back. Everything fits, nice and warm and snug, in their new functional, approaching modern, post-war kitchen: stove against cabinets, varnished white oak pantry in wall, gray Formica laminate table in nook, Gerry at sink or stove, and Robert wherever. In an hour or so, two boys sit or stand on chrome and emerald colored vinyl kitchen chairs.

Robert leans back from table, facing nook, his back to kitchen where Gerry prepares breakfast. He opens *The Birmingham News,* "Sunday Thanksgiving Holiday Edition", November 25, 1951. A big turkey tops its front page. He reads in an intense way as he reads everything from sports to Shakespeare. He grew up dirt farmer poor, in money terms, and print, along with radio and an occasional motion picture, offer conduit for outside influences and a passage out and away—from Depression, from living country, from all-too-common local ignorance, and from himself. He might have been poor, but he and his ancestors strove to excel, took pride in independence, ached at life's inequities, and Robert struggles like the devil to be more—despite himself and others.

He begins to skim and scans news, details for later. He wants to get to station early. His name stands high on the Extra Board list—a list of next in line fireman and engineers to fill any open position caused by changes of scheduled trains and crews. He knows his name tops today's list, and he knows a second—an oddity—an early afternoon passenger train goes out to Meridian and New Orleans today. He sees himself on it, no doubt. He received preliminary notification, he just needs confirmation, from the Call Boy, giving him his call time.

He sits with a certain noticeable, old-fashioned dignity, leans way back in his kitchen chair, sets his newspaper down, and lights his pipe. Life feels good. He takes a few puffs of Sir Walter Raleigh's finest, without inhaling, rests folded hands on his chest, opens his mouth in a wide oval shape and releases a smoke ring—small and defined it floats from his mouth as if blown by a bubble maker. He moves his cheeks just a tad and out comes Ring Two, a bit smaller than his first. Two rings drift, one behind other, still perfect but getting larger and larger and a bit thinner and finally bending and twisting. He lets go Smoke Ring # Three, then Four, takes a puff, then releases two more. Six rings now hover, glide, and fill kitchen —younger ones as circular ring clouds ideal in shape, motion, and direction—older ones decrepit, aimless, beaten by air current, but big enough to put your arms and head through. A sudden move by Gerry doing dishes, and all rings go into disarray, disaster—breaking apart and dispersing into pieces and disconnected segments. As she walks to her Frigidaire, smoke designs reach oblivion.

Gerry's fridge stands five feet with rounded shoulders and one door. She puts a box of open baking soda way back in on an upper shelf to eliminate any odor and rubs her fingers over flaky, soft ice along its interior sides, "I'll defrost it while you're gone." She plops its door closed, turns, and darts back to sink.

Still kicked back in his chair, Robert inspects residual smoke and nibbles his pipe's well chewed bit. He stares down, as if intent on knowing all there is to know about what lies below hard floor and beyond tight walls.

A rotary phone, sitting near his back on counter, gives two long rings, their party line ring. Robert starts from his trance, reaches back and around, and answers before it has a chance to sound again. He spends long phone hours and enjoys union and company discussions. One of his cronies, Red Duncan, who started with the railroad just before him and stands one up in seniority, became a union local chairman, a representative and claim settlement position. Red considers Robert capable of such roles and more.

To phone out or answer Robert stands, to converse he sits.

"Hey, boy," Robert greets the Call Boy. "Why natch', I'm ready and waiting always. Okay, got ya', Boy, Second 47 at 1:15, out 1:45. Consider it done." He listens and roars a big laugh and wide smile—natural, charming, endearing, and handsome despite imperfect teeth, normal for his time and typical post-Depression. "Yeah, Boy, you tell ole Red, when you talk to him, to keep his Caddie—

you know, he's got a new one, bright red color just like he is—tell him to keep top down and everything in good order. I'm looking forward to taking a spin with him when I get back. Yeah, boy, much obliged." He hangs up and clasps hands above head, interlocking fingers, face flushing to think about Red. He leans back again, a shock of curly dark hair piled high. He radiates confidence, people like him. Again thoughtful, perhaps pensive and contemplative, he returns to moving his unlit pipe between thin lips.

He pulls out Hamilton—7:54. *Everything moves a snail's pace on holiday weekend in New Orleans. Almost an hour after originating on time in French Quarter, Train #48, labors across Lake Pontchartrain's north bank nearing Slidell. Restricted speed rules every section: heading out of station; across narrow streets and alleys; near shallow and soggy soiled cemeteries; along iron fences; past aboveground granite tombs, marble mausoleums, and chapels; through close-to-track neighborhoods of white-frame, one-story houses and small red brick businesses; and, over the Southern Railway Bridge, longest in country—seems like world, they say—God's Own Bridge. Out there on a single track, above water and marshland, wakeful adults scan for dry land but see murky, brackish waves, dense swamp, and U. S. Highway 11 tagging along beside.*

A top of line streamliner, The Southerner northbound cruises slow, babies sleep, and passengers observe. A fancy dining car serves five-star breakfast on white tablecloths, attendants pour hot coffee from pure silver serving pots, and porters light big fine cigars for folks.

Music rides on trains. Rhythmic sounds of squeaking springs, steel knocking on steel, and clicking of wheels passing over seams in track support it. Rocking motion and time perpetuate it. Andy Griffith described folk music as true stories set to music. Lore lives on, accuracy on occasions notwithstanding. Johnny Cash, Ernest Tubbs, Griffith and countless songsters covered "The Wreck of Old

97", a traditional legendary tale of a 1903 fast mail train in Virginia whose Southern Railway engineer received orders to put her into Spencer on time.

Gerry pulls a rubber drain stopper, begins drying dishes, places her dish towel down, and scurries back to bedroom. Over her shoulder, she bids to no one in particular, "I need to get out of this darned robe—get presentable." She unbuttons a drab quilted, pink nylon robe her mother gave her.

Robert, ready and dressed, crosses his legs—lost in his Sunday paper: Candidate Eisenhower will promise end to Korean War; Truman again explains how bombs on Japan saved many lives; Alabama amendments to define requirements to register to vote and application of poll taxes; stalemate and peace talks in Korean conflict drag on with no end in sight; nuclear bomb tests and explosions in Nevada and New Mexico; a test rocket intercepts an airplane for a first time; Alabama's November tornadoes and record low November temperatures as far south as Mobile; and "Paint Your Wagon" completes its second week of stage performances in New York City.

In pencil on his paper's margin, he doodles a couple of lines, draws @, and writes 1:15, his call time.

He reads on and saves details of stories for later, perhaps in the crew dressing and locker rooms at station before his departure. He jumps immediately to sports page stories: Chicago first baseman Chuck Conners; all-star MVP favorites Yogi Berra and Roy Campanella; Browns versus Bears; and finally, story of most importance, Florida defeats Red Drew's Alabama. He spent Saturday afternoon listening on radio, disappointed and disgusted. Robert's cousin and nephew play for Alabama. It's big.

Gerry, hair brushed and dressed in part, comes back to kitchen. Robert tells her, "I need another cup of 'fee-'fee." Robert plays words, shortening them and rearranging letters, forming new ones, some clever and some his silly or annoying intention.

Gerry brings her Comet pot over and pours—black and steamy—and returns it to burner.

He evaluates cup and saucer a few seconds, "I said, I wanted a cup of coffee." Robert's words, when serious, come slow, deliberate, and considered.

She looks puzzled and, without an answer, quizzical.

"I said I wanted 'a cup' of coffee." Again, his low voice emotionless and calm yet stern, emphasizing "a cup". He points to the rim of his cup where coffee may only reach three-quarters or seven-eighths its brim.

Gerry stares wide-eyed at him, her brows raised. She takes a deep breath, gnashes a tooth or two, and almost shakes her head— still searching for reason. She walks a few steps, grabs her pot again, takes a few strides to his right side, and pours and fills without saying a word or showing any sign.

His cup runneth over. Hot java splashes around his cup's top and droplets trickle down sides. Robert evaluates and simulates a smirk, his pot of hot 'fee-'fee walks away.

A time comes, after reflection, somewhere down a road, when she wishes she poured it all in his lap and put her hot pot there. She would think back on herself and see herself as stupid, a young, happy, naïve girl—a kid. Gerry had reached 28, but with time, she will see her early life, and many if not most of her generation's, as unwise, unworldly, and uninformed. She grew up on a small city street across from her high school, only out of Alabama a few times by train, married at 19. People traveled and ventured little, but Robert took her by train to New Orleans honeymooning and again by rail to Pasadena to visit his half-brother. She considers Robert older, now 33, well-read, a Marine, a hard worker and good provider, but at times, from their first meeting on, as strangely quiet a person as she ever knew. Still water runs deep, she theorizes.

But on this day in 1951, she keeps her mouth closed.

Gerry exits kitchen, pulls hair back—real tight, washes face, and prepares to take him to station. They will not be late.

At his table, Robert gobbles breakfast, sips his cup of joe, and sops up spilt coffee. If Gerry ate, she stood and moved or dashed around kitchen.

She avoids making excuses for Robert—or her—or anyone—but considers his origin. His mother called his father "Mister." His parents respected each other, both stood and walked tall together with pride, but times and eras stand alone, different and unique. To judge one by another's standards imposes values, customs, mores, and conclusions upon diverse premises and different and often conflicting conditions.

Robert fiddles with his Hamilton, taking appropriate care to inspect and appreciate his grand circle of time—his ring of chapters. Tiny black, rectangular flecks divide hours into minutes, and every minute carries an alternating blue, black, or red dwarfish Arabic numeral with each tenth minute enlarged tenfold in black. Secure and protected, his 21-jewel movement watch face, as much flawless art as unfailing absolutism, lies seated beneath a clear unscratched, resilient, dustproof crystal. Delicate lanceolate hands point out minutes, defining time. He marvels in its fine design and veiled feminine grace. Near lower extreme of face, in center, a diminutive second hand, less than size of a lousy dime, ticks out each precise second. For whatever reasons, Robert admires stateliness at every opportunity, seeing intricacy, integrity, and unfettered human achievement. He takes a last morning acknowledgement of perfection, chuckling aloud, An iron horse.

Autumn turns dry and clear down South, sunlight bright, glaring, and misleading. Robert's quaking index finger and thumb pinch his pocket watch's knurled winding knob, atop stem and casing, and he winds. A scattering of light through his kitchen window shines over Geraldine's sink and reflects off his chronometer's crystal. In one instant, a long blinding one, his watch's entire universe of uncompromised balance becomes lost, but only for a second.

He tilts Hamilton a little, makes sure he sees it right—getting on toward mid-morning—8:53. *Fifty-three miles from its origin and already a couple of minutes late, 48 passes into Pearl River County, Mississippi and through a town called Picayune—a native American word meaning trivial or little value, and also name of a coin, half value of a real. Randy Newman, composer and singer, lived some of his early life in New Orleans. He surmised, generally speakin', they call the paper down here The Picayune, no one from around here ever came to no good, and they still say to this day, hey, New Orleans won the war. Newman did an album and song called "The Dixie Flyer", a train taking his mother and him from LA to New Orleans. The actual Dixie Flyer ran southeastward, Chicago to Florida. So it goes.*

Forty-eight, The Southerner, rolls on.

Departure for station will come hours earlier than needed. Robert's tan, two strap handled, leather travel bag sits by door, prepared and ready to go.

Gerry continues to ready herself and kids. They always howl to go to station, to watch their father walk in and disappear into Terminal Station's side tunnel but being Thanksgiving weekend, she will drop them at Grandpa's and Grandma's, "It's right on our way," and besides, Grandpa's got TV.

Robert feels a bit big, sporty, and extra special. He goes out first and opens a loud creaking steel door on his black 1950 Dodge pickup. He steps on his small running board and into his new design pilot cab. Vehicles sport square angles, steep curves, few aerodynamics, and heavy steel. Robert's truck's finish looks new but flat. His bed sits low with deep walls. "DODGE" covers most of his tailgate in ten-inch bold raised, same color letters. He positions himself behind his shiny, gray, hard plastic steering wheel, almost two feet across with horizontal tilt, as if driving a bus. He grabs on, gets a feel of it, back and forth, and its play. He swells. Most wheels he knew growing up—he didn't know many—felt like wood and drove as if a wagon. He doesn't long for power steering, first time he's ever owned any kind of new steering.

Time to warm her up a little. His key with green SR—Southern Railway insignia—chain slides into ignition switch, located below and midpoint a basic chrome Mopar AM radio centered on his pickup's black steel dashboard. He gives his key a turn, and she starts, sputters, and dies. Again, with his right hand, he reaches down beside his steel steering column and pulls out a chrome knob "THROTTLE". He pulls it out, wide open, and tries it again. His Dodge moans, objects and bangs a little, sputters some, catches, and purrs. A slight victorious grin tightens his smooth skin and cheeks. Again, he thinks, Iron horse, ignoring a few body rattles and engine knocks here and there, common in 1950's autos.

He toots horn, requesting audience.

Other than a hand brake and hood latch, all controls lie in his dash's center except one. Robert uses his left hand to push up a simple chrome heat lever. He pushes to "Hi" to fend off mid-morning cool. Left of his steering wheel, a row of tennis ball sized, white needled gauges keep him apprised of RPM's, oil pressure, and voltage. Centered below in a most conspicuous place, a single, same-size gauge's needle vibrates a fuel reading.

Robert blows again—several beeps—revs 95 horses, and snaps on country. Music hath charms, poet Congreve told us centuries ago, to soothe a savage breast, to soften rocks, to bend a knotted oak. He loves quotes. He wallows in them. 'Tis his nature, as he sees it.

Kids come out next, stand in middle of a plain black leather bench seat, and Gerry jumps in by door. They're off—down Willow Lane. They go a couple of blocks to highway and turn left by Willow Leaf Motel, unostentatious ma and pa operation, popular before interstates.

Toward town, U. S Highway 11 south becomes First Avenue, main drag through city, as they parallel in rough fashion the Southern's mainline along valley floor. They pass a lingering honky-tonk since prohibition, the Silver Slipper. Gerry and Robert went there —considered way out on highway—years before. She remembers dancing and sipping soda with her group in 1941—barely 18—more with Robert's brother Brad, Robert freelancing with no one in particular. She still thinks it good her daddy didn't know where she was. The Slipper, as they called it, had white plank walls, stood one rectangular story, and rested on blocks every five feet or so. A green shingle lean-to roof had a slight slant. A plywood sign displayed Coca-Cola's big red and white scripted traditional logo, bookended by large white coke bottle likenesses. Bold, black print announced **Silver Slipper** and invited **Dine and Dance**. Inside, in 1941, they heard local musicians and singers cover "Wabash Cannon Ball", "Waiting for a Train", "Chattanooga Choo Choo", and yes, "Wreck of Old '97". They listened to songs made famous by Gene Autry who worked in a railroad tower before becoming a singer.

Gerry, as they drive past, revisits memories of friends and good times and again assesses her and her contemporaries' innocence and lack of sophistication. We were lambs to slaughter, thinking of Pearl Harbor and war. Many boys she went to school with never came home.

Late November in Appalachian foothills means groves of rusty auburn, burnt orange, and scarlet. Red oaks, chestnut oaks, sourwood, maple, ash, basswood, and hickories cover foothills. City streets line with yellow and brown shade trees: slippery and winged elm, hackberry, sugarberry, imported chestnut, and maybe a rare American chestnut or American elm, spared by 20th century blights.

Birmingham lies in Jones Valley at an intersection of two metamorphic processes, each eroded and worn down over almost 300 million years by water, wind, light, heat, and cold—much older than California's Eddy Gulch. East and south, a ridge and valley process associated with the Appalachians pushes mountains upward. Soluble rocks, soil, minerals, and elements wash or blow away, and even sandstone, least erodible of all, breaks and tumbles down to valley floors. North and west, a similar process exists but of mountains with more flattened, level sandstone tops—Cumberland Plateau.

Trees cover almost everything in Alabama, but even in 1950's, forest removal takes a toll.

As they pass, Gerry checks out a little burger, pop, beer, and music place called the Chateau, a white ceramic looking building more filling station than restaurant. They ate there a couple of nights before, danced a number or two, and their boys slid a silver disc down a rudimentary style bowling machine with flashing lights and buzzers and bells galore. A jukebox, nonexistent in 1940's Silver Slipper days, played new releases by Hank Williams, "Hey, Good Lookin'" and Gerry's fave "Why Don't You Love Me". Ole Hank laments lack of huggin' and kissin' and wonders why his gal don't love him and spark him like she used to do and say sweet nothin's like she used to coo. Yee-ha, generally speaking. She loves it and speculates, doesn't everyone.

Youngest son mentions how good a doughnut might be. Word has it a new place plans to open soon on left—Krispy Kreme. Robert asks, "Want a Drispy Dreme no-dut?" They remain silent but marvel at limitless word games.

Robert pops his 3-on-column into third, hits gas, and swings into left lane. Gerry throws her left arm out as kid security. They pass East Lake, a 200-acre lake built for real estate development purposes in late 19th Century. On this day, it exists as a shady park and a few amusement rides.

They buzz alongside an overhead electric bus or trolley bus, top half painted white and bottom half dull gold, also headed to town. Older brother informs younger, speaking of Gerry's paternal uncle, "That's what Uncle Paul drives," and points to something like a city bus of future decades but powered by two trolley poles on its roof, connected and forming a circuit above with electrical lines hanging from power poles.

Their kids chatter about East Lake fishing, picnics, and roller coasters, and look east to try to see Ruffner Mountain Fire Tower, highest point on Red Mountain's ridge. From over 1,300 feet, a person gets 360 degrees of city, forests, surrounding coal field, hills and plateaus to north and west, and mountains to east and south. They hike up from home sometimes. An old codger caretaker wakes in his underwear—stuck to his rectum—and talks changing times. He lets them go up, and they get a bird's eye view of central Alabama.

Ruffner Mountain, more than any place along Red Mountain, remains woods. Only a quarry blemishes it, for most part. Titmice, chickadees, cardinals, blue jays, wrens, hawks, owls, and small mammals take refuge and thrive. A tiny stand of mountain variety longleaf pine, near its northern most range, clings to life.

Red Mountain's ridge, including Ruffner Mountain, forms a divide between Jones Valley's Warrior River watershed on one side and Shades Valley's Cahaba River drainage on another. On top of Red Mountain, as with any divide, less than an inch determines how a drop of rainwater travels to ocean—exposing each drop to unique detours, falls, and dead ends.

Robert cruises 30 MPH and better, as their quivering softball sized speedometer tells it. Its dial ranges 0 to 80—needle unsteady any speed. He pushes her past library and a neon pink pig barbecue sign with moving swine legs and feet. He mashes his foot down for 50.

"Robert." His heavy toe lifts a little at Gerry's dissuasion—her extended left arm still holds boys back in seat.

He lets her settle back down around 30, speed limit, as they go by a shake and malt drive-in called the Polar Bear, a sprayed white concrete small ice castle, or big igloo, and canopy covered with sprayed white concrete icicles and a matching polar bear on top—cool and crazy then or now. Gerry thinks of her brother who worked there as a teen. While moving a black, white-walled '39 Studebaker for management, he took "drive-thru" at face value, plowed a support and took out two icicles and gave its polar bear a permanent tilt, negating any of his short tenure's earnings and terminating his employment. Gerry sympathizes, Poor Freddie.

From there, they only need about eight or ten more blocks to reach her parents' house. When those additional blocks disappear, they stop at a red light in front of Woodlawn High School, where Gerry graduated in 1941—proud as can be. WHS, built in 1921, rises as three rectangular stories of brick and ceramic style. Early 20th Century schools contain red brick, mortar, concrete, abundant windows, but maintain Gothicism: intricate detail, trim, design, grand frontal staircase and a few gargoyles guarding up top along roof's edge. Gerry and friends once estimated over 3,000 window-panes in WHS.

At Georgia Road, they career right for a long block below a silver pinnacle steeple of Woodlawn Baptist Church, where Grandma goes almost daily, beside Woodlawn Elementary School, again three brick stories but built earlier, in 1900, a simplistic, square, old brown building in comparison.

Right on 55th Street, and they see Grandma's and Grandpa's house, a block and a half down, directly across from WHS's 4,000-plus seat stadium. They race up in front and cross-park, engine knocking, under crowns of two majestic trees: a huge, 45-inch diameter willow oak with linear, lanceolate, persistent leaves and a fast shedding, compound leaved pecan tree, about half width of its colossal companion.

Grandma and Grandpa keep brown leaf piles in neat, impeccable fashion regardless of any disturbance—wind, human, mechanical, or otherwise. They maintain their modest house and its goldish brown shingle-like siding and gable roof, manicure its small front yard of Bermuda grass of maybe 900 square feet, and sculpt red-berried holly hedges. Grandma vows always, "Don't want to be trashy." The Goodyears clean their furnishings and fashions, Victorian and antiquated, and uphold their lives—regimented, upright, and moral.

Grandpa likes to cuss, but "What the hell." Grandma hears a plenty but talks clean and knows more euphemisms and euphemistic remodeling than most regular churchgoers ever dream.

Gerry gets out with boys and trots them up their grand-parents' 25-foot-long spotless walk. She wears a violet wool top and matching snug skirt with black flat shoes, her hair fixed and wavy, with reasonable makeup for a Sunday. Dark, vibrant colors accentuate and contrast with her skin and hair. She gets her share of lookers and admirers. She walks fast, her kids keep up. She holds younger brother's hand and has older one in sight as they climb three concrete steps by a banister and onto a battleship gray painted porch with three-foot high solid wall railing. White and taupe metal awnings jut out a few feet on all sides except one—near steps and front door where a neighbor's house sits close. Porch design, around turn of 20th century, long before air condition, allow for open air flow on all sides and facilitate socialization and conversation with neighbors and passers-by—something done often in those days.

From his truck, Robert watches Gerry greet her father and go inside and listens as their wooden front screen door bangs closed, followed by a separate bang of each boy. Her adoptive father, Sherrod Eugene Goodyear, sits in a metal armchair. He might look more than 66. All Gerry's life, neighborhood kids called him "Old Man" as a nickname and term of endearment. He too works railroad, at various yards around Birmingham as a train wheel inspector—a lot of bending, standing, foot pounding, and ill weather. He walks to and from streetcar lines each day. His parents immigrated, Gerry never quite got straight from where and when, but his name changed at some point in his early youth from Goodger to Goodyear.

Robert gets out and takes a step or two up their sidewalk to a spot where, by custom, people—friends, acquaintances, businesspeople, and strangers—stand under shade trees to converse with Mr. and Mrs. Goodyear.

"You goin' out, Bob?" Grandpa always dressed in an unstarched, long-sleeved white shirt, dark brown trousers, and black tapered but squared toed, loosely laced, well shined oxfords. Today, he wears a brown vest to match, maybe it being Sunday.

"Yes, sir, Eugene, I am. Out at 1:45 to Meridian."

Eugene scrutinizes Robert, stands, pulls out his own railroad man's Hamilton. He glances at it, returns it to his vest's side pocket, and sits back down in chair—9:52. *Forty-eight, coming out of a long stretch of sandy coastal plain pasture and longleaf pine country, arrives in Hattiesburg. University of Southern Mississippi students and*

others return home from holiday trips, the Big Easy and beyond. Being
still a few minutes late, she only stops for a short pause, time to load and
unload, before whistling twice and burning on northeastward through
upper coastal plain, mixed pine-hardwood forest, and old fields etched
with wagon rutted roads.

Robert tilts head back to consider Eugene's mammoth trees,
his departure hours away. He turns and stares over Woodlawn's
football field, past its stadium, toward Wood Cemetery, older than
Birmingham, where early Woodlawn plantation families of the
early and mid-19th century lie, names like Wood itself, Tarrant,
and Waldrop. He moves back to his truck and jiggles his left rear
taillight—loose a little, a nut needs tightening. Upon completion
using a key for screwdriver, he marches up front and takes a big
clean orange rag, found everywhere around railroad facilities, from
truck to put a little elbow grease on his hood ornament, a ram
precursor with visible horns and head but flattened, contoured, and
streamlined compared to Dodge's upright ram head, recognizable
on models of later decades.

His chassis rides high above its wheels, making him look
spiffy. Robert gives his back left tire a friendly boot for effect and
Eugene's benefit.

"She's looking good, Bob," Eugene observes, still porch sitting,
"but remember, walking ain't crowded."

"Oh, I do, Eugene. You know I do. I grew up in St. Clair
County," Robert smiles and blows air threw his nose as if amused
by his condition and self—his head bobbles. "I know all about walking. And you're right, it sure isn't crowded. It sure isn't." Eugene
nods once.

Gerry comes out alone, "Daddy, I'll be back after I take Robert
to the station. Mama's got Thanksgiving goodies."

Robert stands by his door as Gerry scoots around to her side to get in.

"See ya', Bob," rings out in something known as porch hollering, but only a decibel or two louder than a strong speaking voice.

Robert looks back to their porch, as he steps in his truck, "Yes, sir, Eugene. You take care, Mr. Goodyear."

Their pickup zips farther north down 55th, sweeps a quick turnaround half-circle at a next intersection, and clatters by Eugene, Gerry waving. Their chrome, saucer-like hubcaps, round and spinning fast, reflect late morning southern sun.

Eugene continues to sit on his porch listening to returning quiet.

Robert's ear for music and hearing, in general, remains a little in question. He adjusts his dial as they drive, punching one of five channel select buttons to tune out a church service and choir, then Rosemary Clooney, and tunes in on Paul Harvey's short lived Sunday show. Harvey squeals, "Stand by for news!" as he did for decades on weekdays but first peddles today's recommendation or tip—on this good day, a new treatment for the bursitis.

Gerry says, "Turn it up. Mrs. Street suffers with it so."

Robert turns a chrome volume knob, up then down and it settles about where he started. He feels "proud"—first auto radio he ever owned.

At First Avenue, stopped at a red light, Gerry checks out Woodlawn Methodist, an early century church, on her right—all gray limestone brick, stained glass, gables—and she dips her head down to twist face up for a view of its corner bell tower above. They turn right and west past post office and streets and houses of people Gerry knows, kids from school days and her mama's friends from church.

Thirty city blocks sound far, but a trip from Woodlawn's 55th Street to Birmingham's Terminal station involves few lights and little traffic, especially on Sunday, as First Avenue shoots straight through town's old, industrial section, adjacent to valley floor rail lines.

After about ten blocks, they cross sidetracks serving factories and warehouses. Houses give way to shot houses, then shanties.

Conversation between Gerry and Robert diminishes to as low as it ever gets, as their little journey evolves. Muteness prevails. They cruise past loading docks and storage areas to their left and Avondale Mills, a multi-state cotton mill's headquarters, on their right. Another block or so, and they reach 34th Street and ascend half mile long First Avenue Viaduct, built to span steel center, boom town railroad tracks, and iron manufacturing cooling water. To their left, below and beside viaduct, stands Sloss Furnace's massive and rust red stacks, coned shaped boilers, storage tanks, belts, smoke, steam, ash, sparks, spraying water, and a huge ladle car pouring molten liquid so hot, red, and bright, it hurts eyes. Cars pull over along The Viaduct in short-term viewing lanes designed for people wanting to look down into a state-of-the-art pig iron making process—it doesn't get any better.

To their right, a few blocks away, Birmingham's Terminal Station becomes visible, looking distant and mystic and removed, as if a temple.

Robert puts her into neutral and coasts off The Viaduct's west end—saving gas, engine, clutch, or something.

At 26th street, they whip right, crawl a couple more blocks, creep in front of the station, and inch to a halt at north end parking —ignition already off.

"When will you be back?" She would meet him.

"Extra-board today. I'll deadhead back tomorrow on 42, same time as always."

She knew 42 came in early. She'd call the Call Boy, find out if it was on time, and be there well before train arrival, as suitable and expected.

He gets out, she slides over. He remembers through her open window, "Oh, that nosey ole woman on the party line keeps picking up on our ring. She knows it. I've tried to tell her to mind her own damn business, but she picks up and listens all the time."

Gerry agrees, "She does it to me too. Poor thing. Must not have enough to do and think about."

"Call the damned phone company," he raises his shoulders, "and tell them to do something about her."

"They can't do anything, Robert. We don't have private service that far out where we live. They can't do anything."

"Well, hell, Mama, call them anyway. Just call 'em." He takes a few steps, turns back to her, and adds, "If you'd just do what I tell you."

She thinks, why don't you call them, and I'm not your mama, but says, "I will," and considers, I might.

Robert grabs his travel bag from truck bed. He wears work clothes—slate blue shirt, brown work shoes, and those olive pants, from his hangar, on his closet, at home this morning, before crack of dawn.

He arrives Terminal Station two hours and forty-four minutes early and confirms by his dangling Hamilton—10:31. *Past a momentary station stop, 48 clears a yellow-pine sawmill and lumberyard, separated from the track right-of-way by a swamp and shrub thicket of bushes with evergreen, aromatic elliptical leaves and purple drupes. Folks call it, and anything like it, laurel.*

Laurel, Mississippi

A loaded logging truck cuts it way too close getting over a muddy, unimproved crossing—48's whistle howls.

Robert walks toward a tunnel leading through the station's north end, past a waiting area, and turns into a crew dressing room area. At call time, he and other crew members appear out back, near tracks, and walk across a level area, where tracks and walkway are flush, to their track and train. His train, Second 47 wasn't due in from Atlanta until 1:35, ten minutes before departure. If their kids had come, they like this part. Sometimes, they walk in with him and over by tracks. Today, he walks alone and out of sight.

Gerry pulls her skirt above her knees. "This blasted seat's still back," to herself, "darn it." She struggles with her jammed truck bench for going on a minute or two—who's counting.

Robert left his engine off—the thing to do.

"Let's get this flivver up and running," again under her breath. She turns ignition, but it misses. Gerry pulls out its throttle halfway, tries it, but nothing. Pushes it back in, stretches to push down gas all the way, and hits it again. "Here we go," with her hands going up into air.

She cranks her radio. Red Foley's #1 folk chart hit "Birmingham Bounce" blares from a single speaker, antiquated in today's manicured sound realm but cutting edge by 50's standards. She responds, "I like that beat"—more undiscovered rock than ubiquitous country. Some call this song first rock 'n' roll.

Gerry pops her clutch—by accident—and her Dodge truck shoots forward four feet or so. "Oh, Geraldine," she mutters and laughs. "Look out, Lucky Teter," thinking of an old stunt driver, Lucky Teter and His Hell Drivers—greatest daredevils and stunt car group ever, said radio and posters and spectators at carnivals and fairs.

Gerry gains control of her ride again, and off she goes toward her parents' house, promenading a half block or so and struggling with both hands, one over her steering wheel and one under, to turn her big, stiff wheel. She loops back east into Fifth Avenue's underpass, a major city street below the entire Terminal Station and all its dozen or so tracks crossing, north and south, above. In front of her lie over two football fields of smooth underground boulevard disappearing into a tiny circle of light at tunnel's far end. In her rearview mirror, a big three-story cast iron electric sign facing station fades away—Birmingham~The Magic City.

Gerry's radio fuzzes out giving her quiet time to talk to herself and sort, "He's good—a good man, good to me and the kids." Her hair blows in breeze, and she shakes her head, thinking about their morning coffee episode, "But, he can be a huge horse's ass." She looks out her side view mirror, sees it all clear, and hits her gas. "And, true, he can get a snootful sometimes, if not too often. But he's good, smart, handsome, a good provider—not rough really, in any way, at all. Not really mean. Actually, he's a pushover. And he's fun sometimes, in spite of himself." She sums and sympathizes, "Poor Robert."

Gerry loves her life, her family, her starter home, her husband. She has a fragile grasp on what she wants.

As she clears tunnel, her radio rejuvenates—first static and then fanfare and an important announcement: Santa has just arrived (via Cincinnati) on *The Hummingbird* at the L & N (Louisville & Nashville) station, a few blocks away. Maybe next week when Grandma takes boys to town by streetcar to motsey around, as her mama calls it, they can go see Santa.

Gerry changes channels and picks up Nat King Cole, born in Montgomery, singing "Too Young", a song of young lovers starting out and proving old doubters wrong. No one can sing it like Nat, she reckons. Alabama fellas just have it.

Activity and optimism abound—for Geraldine, the South, and a post-war world. She traverses a different way back to her parents' home.

Growing up, as kids on Willow Lane, we spun 45, 78, and 33 vinyl records. We picked guitar and sang about everything singable, even tragedy and trains. "The Wreck of Old 97" warned: Never speak harsh words, he may leave and never return.

3

Casey Jones Hand on Throttle

Robert likes his early arrivals at station. It gives him time to wander and ponder, maybe shake a hand or two. For a guy who at home mixed pesky, cutting humor and strange quiet, his unrestrained and endless charm exudes in public. Earlier than even usual, he roves station. Maybe, things at home made him feel confined or static or edgy. Maybe he likes to roam, travel, adventure unknown, a local country boy still escaping confining beginnings. He finds it difficult to put a finger on, but he tries. He always tries to calculate in every endeavor. His mind moves in a controlled mode. Unlike Gerry, Robert dislikes leaving things to chance.

Robert exits a crew locker room and takes a concrete corridor along back side of station. He often goes this way, through a seldom used entrance to frequent a newsstand—awaiting call time. He strains to open a stuck forgotten side door of huge, thick green wood and glass and steps into a waiting area clamoring with Thanksgiving travelers—bustling, pushing, shouting, talking, laughing.

Birmingham's Terminal Station dwarfs him. He imagines a hollow European cathedral, bigger than ever seen in pictures. Sounds echo and time recoils. An ornate, rounded, expansive dome above, maybe 100-feet high or more and 60 or 70 wide, humbles him every time. Today resonates louder—a frenzied holiday weekend. Pigeons, way more than usual by his calculation, flap and hover in beams and braces, high up in rafters. Facing upward, he estimates, Must be hundreds or thousands of them.

Robert twirls his gold watch chain a time or two—11:47. *In Meridian, Mississippi, two blocks from white stucco, maroon domed, "Spanish looking" Union Station, train crews from Birmingham overnight at Union Hotel, smaller but similar in style and color. Hickory stick whittling bent men sit out front near hotel entrance. Inside Engineer J. D. Pyler and Fireman C. R. Alass finish made to order breakfast. Busy waitresses and cooks lay out a southern style dinner steamtable served daily of fried chicken country fried steak, mashed potatoes and gravy, black eyed peas, sweet potato casserole with apples and marshmallow, yellow squash and onions, greens, homemade potato salad, piccadilly, pickled watermelon rinds, corn pone, warm banana pudding, steaming coffee, and sweet tea. A sign in window reads: Tuckered Out—and Hungry—Train Crews and Travelers Welcome.*

Pyler and Alass walk out toward station for their three hours plus return trip home. As normal, they came down night before on 41. They hear 48's whistle approaching. Pyler ducks into Union Station's gift shop and picks up The Birmingham News and gives it to Alass. They work together a first time, but both know today's route well, especially Old Man Pyler. Railroad people attract nicknames.

Forty-eight, with Pyler and Alass at controls, departs Meridian six minutes late.

Above Robert, a vast chandelier, a spreading centerpiece to station, suspends from six massive black steel link chains. In it, two glistening brass circles encase incandescent bulbs, a large outer ring of 84 and a smaller inner of 24. He knows people, even adults, who count them. He strolls across two-foot square marble slabs and under stain glass beaconing: FOUNTAIN. Gift shop signs beyond offer reading material, stationary, souvenirs, newspapers, maps, candy. At a magazine rack, he glances over *The Montgomery Advertiser, The Atlanta Constitution, The Times Picayune,* and thumbs a few paperbacks. Lacking sweet tooth, he mostly eyes a cashier who looks Robert's way. Her name remains a mystery. He and Red and some others have discussed her from time to time.

She excuses herself from irritated patrons and comes out from behind counter to retrieve a down-home cookbook from an upper shelf. She reaches long and far, extends way up, and stretches. Her mid-calf skirt pulls up enough to bare knee joint and calf flex—for him, all for him.

Her skin looks fair and her hair light blonde or strawberry. Something feels new and strange about her—different from Gerry who by most accounts looks pretty good. But this girl appears un-explored and sensual—to a traveling man. Her leg muscles ripple in hose, thick for coming winter.

"Her legs," comes from Robert's mouth. He takes out his pipe and pats it on his hand to knock out residual ashes, and he meanders her shop—pacing.

Among railroad knickknacks, Robert sees a diminutive jack-in-the-box entitled Casey Jones American Engineer. He pushes down with a finger and out pops Jack in a traditional fine pin-striped, gray and black, railroad cap. A little wind-up music box within sings in a crackling Spike Jones voice, "Casey Jones, hand on the throttle; Casey Jones, he's a brave engineer. Casey Jones, a great American hero; Casey Jones he's a giant of a man." Casey Jones, as legend had it, died trying to save his passengers when his train smashed a stalled freight in Mississippi. His story, poems, and songs vary among tellers. Spike Jones, a contemporary satirical humorist, sang and spoofed exploits of Casey and others.

Back out in an enormous waiting area, Robert stares up a last time at its ceiling and refocuses, trying to see and wondering about cooing and crowing pigeons—moving like flocks of starlings —but sees mostly light bulbs, skylights, reflection, and slanted late autumn sunlight.

A holiday weekend throng mills around him, many resting on waiting room oak benches resembling church pews. He feels a little guilty, like a philanderer, a potential adulterer.

A live mike pops on PA above and a booming voice announces Illinois Central's *City of Miami* departure for St. Louis and Chicago. Passengers—men dressed to kill in trench coats and matching hats and women in ¾ length dresses hiding under stylish caps and mesh veils—herd toward steps leading to an underground midway, below tracks, to trains. Behind them, they leave gum and candy wrappers, cigar and cigarette butts, spilled soft drink, food particles, and spit chew.

Pigeons above coo louder, a mob thins, and Robert thinks legs.

He detours by an in-house postal office and drops a bill payment. By a waiting room marked Coloreds, a gray bearded Southern porter stands by an entrance, "Do you have time, suh?"

Robert studies, tries to recollect and identify and shows him his Hamilton—12:16.

Forty-eight, crosses out of Mississippi into Alabama at Cuba, almost all black. Some areas and towns existed as slave communities and their demographics show it. The Southerner hums northeast, still trying to make up a little lost time.

Robert begins to remember. Porter William "Willie" Skitts worked railroad, in some capacity, longer than anyone remembers. For going on a decade, he served on *The Southerner,* #47 and #48 between New Orleans and Washington, DC. He rode and stayed in Pullman sleeper cars, turning down beds, moving baggage, serving food and snacks, greeting and assisting passengers, keeping things tidy for pay and tips. If a Pullman bedroom passenger, at bedtime, put shoes in a wall pass thru box, Skitts, as all porters did, picked them up from outside in hall and returned them by morning—waxed and spit shined to a hard, reflective gloss.

Robert knew Skitts as a kind, helpful, proud, ancient man in a high-collared military navy-blue uniform, gold buttoned top to bottom with matching cap, round and two to three inches in height, like a small squat can or drum, with a black bill. He must have been born along about time of Confederacy, Robert and everyone only guess when.

Pullman manufactured railroad cars for over a century, people called a sleeping car Pullman.

"Skitts, I haven't seen you in ages. You going out today? Thought you had quit."

Skitts nods, "They got me going out on that second train." He looked a bit lost.

"Good, that'll be me and Cecil Love to Meridian. I'm Bob."

Robert skims a small waiting area. Floors and tiles appear similar if not identical to "white" areas, but benches sit lower, and fewer globed lamps hang than beyond a thin partition and under a sign designating Whites. To his right, a small electric office clock sweeps a full length red second hand—behind time.

"I gotta go, Skitts. Time's wasting." Porter Skitts nods.

Robert hustles back as he came. He needs to get his orders, grab his bag and go—get out to his train's track. On a list of large, thick chalk written departures and arrivals comprising most of a wall, he notes his train due in at 1:45, ten minutes late from Atlanta.

He checks watch—12:53. *Forty-eight roars through Epes, Alabama, a mostly white town of cotton gins and stockyards, and crosses over Tombigbee River white cliffs, nearly 100 feet high, used for military purposes and defense by everyone from Choctaws and Creeks to France and Britain and Spain to Confederacy and U. S. Many flags flown here.*

At a cramped operator's office, Robert picks up train orders, an updated employee timetable, and timecard.

In his locker's mirror, he checks himself to mixed response. His train a few minutes late, he takes time to shave again. He applies hot water and stirs his natural bristled brush in a thick glass cup. He takes his long-deceased father's straight razor from a natural leather ditty bag, slings it open, and completes his facial improving process. He adds a few drops of cool Ice Blue Aqua Velva from a clear, deltoid glass bottle and emerges renewed. He's ready to roll and thinks, Her legs.

Travel bag straps in hand, Robert takes his time on an outside walkway, flush across tracks, north end of station. Passengers go to and from trains underground and board under extensive sheds but crews either go north or south a short way, depending on where their respective engine stop, and walk outdoors to join their trains. Often, crews stroll together, but today, Robert strides alone. He likes and respects today's engineer, Cecil Love, but considers him elder.

Robert positions himself on Track #8's west side loading platform. He knows an exact spot where his engine stops, all engineers and firemen do.

The Terminal Station lay four or five blocks north of Southern's main line with a one-directional switch for approaching trains. Southbound arrivals head into station, northbounds pass the mainline switch and back up to enter. A reverse holds true for departures, southbounds back out, then go south, and northbounds pull straight out onto mainline and veer north. Robert waits at far—north—end of tracks to board southbound Second 47's engine.

Weather seldom gets better—clear, mild, bright, and crisp in Dixie. From his location, Robert sees an additional dozen or so tracks to his east, away from station, freight tracks for most part. To his west, lies station. Against angling sun, he strains to focus on central dome of station, above where he meandered moments before.

A couple of buddies approach, coming from Track #10. They trudge along, looking bedraggled and feeling forlorn. Each moves as a tortoise, every step a chore.

Robert lifts his right hand and puts on, "Hail to lost ones. O' hail, distressed wanderers."

Quietness returns.

"Oh, hail?"

They maintain silence, take their place beside him in a triangle, and drop their bags with two definite, resounding thumps.

"What brings you sojourners so far on so fine a day?"

"Hey, boy," a red-haired man speaks first, and his companion adds, "Hell, I've plumb had it."

Robert sticks out his hand to the first, "C. W."

C. W. Cottrell shakes, decked out in his dark navy, wool blend uniform, big black buttons, and matching hat—like Skittts's porter attire, but grander, and his suit opens with a white shirt and matching tie. He's identified by a conspicuous gold nameplate on his chest. His hat looks bigger too, more distinguished than a porter's with a higher, wider crown and fine, woven yellow cord around its base. Another reflecting gold plate up front signifies rank and mission: Conductor Southern Railway.

C. W. Cottrell worked with Robert at Conners Steel before the war and his girlfriend, now wife Lucille, lived nearby in Woodlawn and introduced Robert to Gerry. C. W. went to work for the railroad right after the war and told Robert they needed men and suggested Robert apply. C. W. has a prominent, almost bulbous nose and red hair, worn straight back with recession each side, and light, porous skin. He looks Irish. He shakes Robert's hand in warmest of ways.

C. W.'s fellow traveler, Frank Sparks, sticks out his hand, too. "Bob, fancy meeting you here."

Robert shakes his hand too, as before, as amiable as it gets, "Miracles appear in the strangest of places." They throw an arm around each other.

"Where you gentlemen headed?" Robert inquires. He knew they both operated #17 and #18 between Birmingham and Chattanooga. Sparks dresses work-casual in blue resembling mechanic's attire. His facial lines run vertical, his head thin, and hair almost black, short on sides. He tops things off with a bright green Southern "SR" logo on black ball cap which he removes in exasperation over conditions north toward Chattanooga.

Sparks replies, "Aw, hell, we just came in on 17. That damned Chattanooga was all fouled up with traffic and mechanical breakdowns and what have you. I didn't think all those sons-of-bitches," and smiles, "would ever clear out of our way. We're three hours late and no reason for it whatsoever. You know what I mean." He wipes hair, shakes head in disgust, and repositions cap—bill back in haphazard tilt.

C. W. smiles at Robert, "What you doin', son? You must be going out. You waiting on 47?"

"Oui," in character, "partially true. They've got a second train going down today. Cecil Love and I at controls." Robert put both hands in his pockets and looks south. "There's 47." A bright oscillating headlight, something new in daylight in those days, comes up Track 7 some 40 yards from them, and Southern's white and Virginia green diesel locomotive clears the loading shed and roars up at about five miles per hour with brakes squeaking and hissing as she stops, maybe 20 yards shy of their communion.

"How's that?" C. W., curious for detail, speaks louder to get above 47's rumble.

Robert increases his volume over and around engine noise and brake steam bursts, "Track trouble down south, West Point or Montgomery or somewhere. Information is kind of sketchy, a wash out or something. *The Crescent* will be detouring today through here to Meridian—calling it Second 47. Cecil and I will be running ten minutes behind 47, First 47, that is." He gestures at 47, *The Southerner* southbound, idling with workmen going in and out underneath to check functions and passengers congregating up and down its silvery sides.

C. W. picks up his travel satchel, more a large, sharp cornered briefcase than overnighter, as Sparks and Robert use. Conductors deal with public and appearance matters. C. W. moves on toward station, "Well, there's plenty of folks needing a ride today, goin' home. Tell Geraldine hello for me." He—going so far back—uses her full name, as does Robert.

"I will. And same to 'Cillie. How is she?"

"Lucille is fine," C. W. inches back and away to leave.

"Oh, C. W., I saw ole Skitts in there."

"Yeah? Do tell. William. I haven't seen him in—don't know when. They say he's kind of lost his memory and mind and all. No telling how old he is. Been around forever."

"He says he's going to New Orleans today."

"How 'bout that. Time will tell, I suppose."

Sparks picks up his gear and begins to walk away too but talks as he goes, "Get with me when you get back, Bob, I want to talk to you about some things."

"Not about that gal in the gift shop, I hope," C. W. interrupts and laughs.

Sparks looks between the two and grins, "No, hell, no, not about some gal. Ole Red saw her name tag though—says her name is Dinah. Gotta go."

Robert beams and hums low, "Someone's in the kitchen with Dinah—" and confides, "Helen will have your ass."

"Oh, I know," Sparks answers, "and Geraldine yours. I'm not interested. And I wouldn't do anything to harm Geraldine or you and Geraldine—not a thing, not a blessed thing."

Robert responds, "Why sure," and looks down Track #8 for his train.

Sparks looks at his Hamilton, as C. W. walks ahead, and adds, "All kidding aside, the thing I really want to talk to you about is the local chairman job, Bob. You could have won that thing. Now some ass from up in Chattanooga got the position only 'cause you didn't run. Now the local chairman is a pain—"

Robert agrees, "An insipid oaf."

Sparks nods, "Well, run this next time then. You'd be the best at it. I don't want it—not now. Too much going on at home and everything. Besides, you'd be best at it. Maybe someday for me. You do it now. You hold seniority over me anyway. It's just got your name written all over it. Run for it before some, as you said, oaf gets elected again." He leaves, weaving in a slow gait, across an arrow marked walk, station bound, a boxcar length behind C.W. Two better friends a fellow couldn't have.

Robert watches for train and waits. He notices oncoming Engineer Cecil Love and Conductor W. J. Sullivan, his fellow crew members for Second 47 to Meridian. Another familiar looking man at their side matches them step for step from station.

Robert checks time—1:14. *A barge loaded with tree length loblolly pine pulpwood waits as 48, 70 miles southwest of Tuscaloosa, clears a drawbridge over Black Warrior River muddy water.*

Conductor Sullivan greets, "Good to see you, Bob," and goes on down along track to where passengers load and unload under an umbrella shed, shady and dry regardless of conditions.

Robert knows a third man at Cecil Love's side to be a road foreman. Road foremen, or road foremen of engines, ride on trains as a supervisor of engineers. They lack union affiliation and serve to protect company interests and ensure specifications compliance. Often, they worked as engineers before joining railroad management.

Cecil says, "Bob, you do know Road Foreman Sam Pape, don't you?"

Robert replies, "Yes, I do. Hello, Sam, how've you been? We worked a little once up on the north end."

"Yes, that's right, Bob, good to see you again. We came back from Chattanooga once."

"That's true." Robert liked this man. They hit it off well before.

"Excuse me." Pape drops his bag and goes down the track as Sullivan had gone.

Cecil follows, "I gotta say somethin' to Sul', Bob. Be right back. Don't leave without me."

Robert continues waiting. Down track, he watches Conductor Sullivan conversing with Engineer Love. Passengers begin to congregate and mill. Switch engines go up and down tracks, moving and changing passenger cars from one train and destination to another. Out beyond track 10, more activity occurs with freight cars being moved in and out and thru. Some switch engines pass without any cars, moving fast to be in a yard. Switch engines got their name from their primary function switching cars from train to train. They also moved cars around yards and sometimes pulled trains, mostly freights and locals. They look less aerodynamic than lead locomotive engines used on higher speed thru trains, more square, reversible with couples on both ends. To a layman, a switch engine's front looks about like its back, its cab offset to rear a bit. Road engines have rounded fronts and angled setback front windows to reduce wind resistance.

Robert watches his birds around station dome, back in one of his trances, growing eager and impatient—almost time to roll. He walks up and down a few feet with hands on hips. It won't be long now.

Inside, a mic goes live again and the station's P. A. fuzzes until a grating newscaster-like voice comes on, "Attention, passengers, now arriving on Track 8, *The Crescent,* Train No. Second 47, from New York, Washington DC, Charlotte, Greenville, and Atlanta. Now arriving Track 8."

Second 47 barrels in, bright headlight spinning, engine thundering, green and white color gleaming, as they did mid-20th Century. Southern's lead engine diesel locomotives all look sleek and fancy. To a kid, they resemble a *Little Engine Who Could* with a headlight for a nose, divided and slanted windshields for eyes, hourglass shaped snout, even another light and SR insignia, from a distance, forming a mouth. Diesel engines seem to live and breathe to a young observer or idealistic eye much as steam locomotives animated for older generations. Maybe, sleek diesel streamlined trains look something like a hawk in motion or an eagle or leopard or serpent, maybe a racing horse or hound. Their new cars shine and glimmer. Passenger service in America got as good as good gets—so to speak.

PA comes back on, through his nose and loud again, "Attention passengers, now boarding on Track 8, *The Crescent*, Train No. Second 47, with service to Tuscaloosa, Meridian, Laurel, Hattiesburg, Slidell, and New Orleans. All aboard on Track # 8." And then, after a brief pause, in a voice with inflection like a military call to attention, "All aboard!" Most days, this route belongs solely to 47, *The Southerner*. Today, Second 47, *The Crescent*, follows close behind.

Robert prepares to climb his engine's left side ladder. He refers to Hamilton—1:43. *Forty-eight moves on a fast haul, closing time in open country, but slows again by the Black Warrior and coasts past Indian mounds, bigger ones by river and smaller ones eastward, away from water. Prominent people in ancient native American society received burial nearer river. Moundville, Alabama. Once beyond sacred remains, Engineer Pyler hits his throttle for next stop Tuscaloosa.*

Cecil scurries as best he can back up tracks and rejoins Robert, his fireman. Cecil telegraphs years, a bit pale and worn perhaps, his movements slow and deliberate. Everyone loves Uncle Cecil. He wears a tan hunting-style jacket, khaki work pants, and squints at everyone from below a worn striped traditional "USA" railroad cap. He began his Southern Railway service at age 15—and shoveled coal and did other jobs until he became an engineer. He wastes little time and goes straight to Second 47's engine's ladder, where two men, a fireman and engineer from Atlanta, detrain. They work off another district, and Cecil and Robert only knew them in passing. Cecil starts up, taking it slow, one ladder step—with both feet— at a time.

Robert sees little reason to miss a chance to welcome arriving crew members and sticks out his hand, "Bob Gambrell," and turns it on a little about tracks east of town, life in Georgia and Alabama, and their regaining a couple of lost minutes. Everything looks ordinary—nice trip, a day in life. They bid happy trails.

"Much obliged, boys," Robert farewells, he makes people like and remember him.

Wheels on diesel locomotives look like huge steel saucers, maybe three feet across, with springs and brake mechanisms in field (facing out) and a flange which fits inside a rail (in gage) and holds train on track. Diesel locomotives weigh several hundred thousand pounds, span over 20 yards in length, and stand almost three men high. Second 47 has two such units, one facing forward, where Robert and Cecil sit, and one right behind, facing back. Robert stays incredulous of their size, weight, and power and often thinks it over, in general and exact terms. He thrusts his right simple work boot in its first ladder rung and pushes up—each step one and half feet apart. He goes up like a young cat compared to a couple of decades older Cecil and through a door big enough—a tight squeeze —for increasing railroader waistlines enjoying a good life at last. Above his engine's bellowing rumble, he quips, "Mr. Love, I have arrived."

Gray, thinning haired Cecil stands by his seat, above his controls, and with a sober stare straight ahead, "We got a road foreman on here today." He takes off his cap and hangs it on a steel rod nub, protruding from his cab's right wall, intended for hanging lanterns or note boards. Everything on metal walls shake, their idling engines so powerful. Engine parts reverberate and rattle and growl relentless cacophony. You just have to hear over it and through it, best you can. They're used to it.

Robert and Cecil place their belongings in personal storage bins, get comfortable, and prepare to roll. Cecil, as engineer, has a seat on right behind throttle and brakes. Firemen sit left or stand. Another seat aligns between them, only perched a little higher to allow a third person to see over their engine's rounded and protruding nose. Each black leather chair swivels and allows for adjustment, but usually rests on a pedestal approximately three feet in height. Almost six feet separates fireman from engineer. Firemen often prefer to stand, engineers sit. Compartments and controls fill cab. Behind them rides 60 linear feet of diesel engines and generators powering traction motors below which in turn move drive wheels with earth shaking horsepower. Little wonder she makes so much racket.

After a few minutes, "Pape's all right, Cece."

Cecil fails to answer then asks, "How's that?"

Robert watches Cecil finish checking his brakes.

"I like Pape." Robert spoke in an honest and confidential way before turning back into his engine room, examining gauges, meters, levels, and lights.

Shoveling coal became ancient history in Robert's world in five short years. Some requirements changed or disappeared altogether: sweat, grit, muscle, brawn, endurance, a strong back. Some remained constant: attentiveness, vision, clear thinking, communication, judgment, and if lucky, quick action.

Robert comes back up front to where Cecil stands talking to cordial and pleasant Road Foreman S. M. Pape and joins, "Good to be with you again, Mr. Pape. We had a nice ride before when we met, let's do no less today." Robert feigns propriety at every opportunity.

"Yes, sir, Fireman Gambrell, we'll do that. I'll just take my seat here between you and Engineer Love."

Cecil moves far right and settles in his chair behind throttle. He places his Hamilton in a designed molded stand on his "dashboard", visible for him at all times and says in a cordial way, "Bob, Pape is new on this end of the line. We'll have to show him all the sights going down today."

"Yes, sir, Engineer Love, we shall indeed." They all exchange nods and smiles.

Robert stands and watches out left side of engine toward end of train. First 47, having pulled out a short while before, must have been cleared and moved on down the mainline. A flagman gives a wave, and Robert sees Conductor Sullivan shouting, "All aboard" to passengers, "Looks like we're about ready to go, Uncle Cecil." He sees a green signal from a tower controlling station entrance and exit.

Cecil picks up a radio phone, a recent invention, and talks to Mr. Sullivan, back a few cars, who as conductor has ultimate control of "his train"—his cars. Cecil maintains authority over "his engines" and throttle, as did Robert as proxy for his engineer in emergency, however, in normal situations, Mr. Sullivan must give okay from his end. A radio phone, still experimental, worked on signals transmitted through train and sometimes rail. At best, it might work as a short-range walkie-talkie within train or with tower while alongside it, at worst, a person hears nothing and resorts to hand signal, flag, voice, lantern, fusee—all playing roles in governance of trains for centuries.

"Got it, Bob. All clear behind." Cecil sets down his handset and begins slipping on clean beige jersey work gloves. He waits a moment, takes a breath, and relaxes.

His conductor, Mr. Sullivan, confirms their discussion with two sharp, high note signals on overhead buzzer.

Robert confirms, "All clear behind. Proceed, Engineer Love," still looking at flagman and now Mr. Sullivan giving hand signals from behind.

Cecil flips a switch with his right hand to start a loud bell ringing heard over most all platforms and tracks throughout Terminal Station. His left hand pulls down on an overhead cord giving three short blasts on his whistle, ear-splitting to anyone near their engine and heard throughout a large part of the city. And, again with his right hand, he releases his brake control, pauses a second, and his left hand moves his throttle. As they back up, Conductor Sullivan, in back, will handle "the air"—the brake.

Cecil looks at his Hamilton mounted in front of him and Robert at his. Cecil says, "1:55." Robert reiterates in a low voice, "1:55." And after a second, Pape chimes in for sport, just audible, "1:55." *In Tuscaloosa, 48 halts on Greensboro Avenue, a yellow brick one-story station with turret, constructed in early century. University students make up a large portion of detraining passengers. A healthy crowd of 55 board.*

Tuscaloosa sits on a fall line between the Piedmont plateau north and coastal plains south at a Black Warrior River shallow shoal, a natural ford for millions of years.

If you've ever ridden a train, especially yesteryear, you know first movements on occasion arrive in an abrupt way. Slack exists around couplings, between cars, and when immense power accelerates, tightening results with more momentum than engineers hope and intend. So things go November 25. Second 47 lunges backward a couple of feet or so as metal against metal echoes, bangs, and crunches, car to car, as force adds tension up and down train sounding like a stepped-on accordion.

"Careful, Cecil," Robert kids.

"Hold on, men. I got 'er," Engineer Love proclaims with a wide-eyed glance.

Robert, still standing and looking back, affirms, "You got 'er, Cece'."

Mr. Pape, in middle seat, smiles and shuffles a form or two.

Cecil rotates his seat to look back as they reverse. He places his left hand on his throttle—pushing it forward and clockwise a notch or two to accelerate and pulling backward and counterclockwise to slow. His right arm, as most always, rests near his brake. He keeps a foot on his dead man's pedal, resembling a modern automobile brake but wider, chrome plated, and noduled steel. If his foot comes off, his train comes to an abrupt stop.

"Got 'er, gentlemen."

They back, a few miles per hour, out of Birmingham's Terminal Station, on their left, and away from its twin steeple-like towers, noble central dome, and sprawling, ten-track loading area.

In reverse, they ease under First Avenue's viaduct, where Robert and Gerry drove a few hours earlier and through what railroaders call Puzzle Switches, where train lines from all over town cross forming a labyrinth.

Second 47 backs up on Sloss Furnace's south side, away from viaduct, stopping clear of switches to await signals. Sloss sits on right, and Cecil and Robert's and Conductor Sullivan's train faces down a southwestern running mainline.

Cecil says as they stop, "We'll be here a minute." He picks up and looks at a few onion skinned train orders off his dash, and Robert and Pape follow suit with their copies. Cecil continues, "That Seaboard rules the roost here." He stares straight ahead at a white Seaboard Air Line Railway engine, with red horizontal racing stripe, *The Cotton Blossom,* already creeping across mainline and through puzzle switches in front of them, entering station.

"We'll be ten minutes behind 'em." Cecil speaks of First 47, the regularly scheduled train on this route. Robert and Pape knew all this. Cecil adds, "We'll be there."

Alongside, a Southern switch engine pushes three black, loaded gondola coal cars into Sloss. As it passes, three parked dull gray open hopper cars filled with silvery white slag becomes visible on a next track. Coal fuels iron and steel mills, slag a by-product. Low-sided gondola cars and high-sided hoppers, both rectangular, transport loose bulk commodity payload. Lines north through the puzzle serve furnaces and fabrication plants in North Birmingham and, a few miles beyond, Tarrant and Sayreton. Birmingham smokes in day, glows by night.

Robert goes back through a shoulder-wide, inside walk along the left flank, port side, of his engine to observe a gauge in a first compartment. He comes back after only a few seconds and Cecil and Pape chat, so he listens and rejoins them. They talk family, Sloss and iron, and Birmingham's skyline, as it was, in front of them on their right, west of the station. Smoke pours out from Sloss and gives things a dingy, yellowish-brown tint. Steel and iron production sounds become dominant, making more noise than Second 47 —saying something.

Birmingham looks its part, as its English namesake—an industrial, manufacturing leviathan. Three buildings dominate 1951 skyline: John Hand Building, Bankhead Hotel, and Comer Building, all built early 20th Century, with latter being 27 floors, proclaimed tallest in South when built.

"How we doin', Pape?" Cecil jousts.

Pape understands, "Oh, I don't know. We'll be okay." He looks in a pleasant way to each man on both sides.

"Agreed." Robert says.

Cecil concurs, "Me too. Can't argue."

Robert sees Pape as a good man, nondescript, and mild. Or maybe Robert sees Pape as a company man—nothing more, nothing less.

"We'll be here a few minutes," Cecil repeats. "That L&N's gotta clear up there too." He flips his index up as to point up ahead to another train now crossing through the puzzle, a L&N passenger train heading north, past the Terminal Station, heading for Nashville. In front of them, an L & N installed metal, iron pipe gate blocks their mainline south.

Cecil just keeps air and mind clear by stating obvious.

Another switch engine chugs alongside moving coke around furnaces on their right. Behind them on their left, nearby and a few blocks away, the Southern operates engine facilities and round-houses with parked engines cars being stored, repaired, and maintained. Everything bustles.

As they wait for clearance and a red signal to change, Cecil continues to make conversation, "Bob, don't forget ole Pape's new around here. We gotta keep him up to snuff. He's a Yankee," Cecil chortles—a loud, long warm one.

Robert comes back in a calm way, "Is that right? We will. Yes, indeed, we will."

Pape corrects, "Not a Yankee but Civil War history interests me and same goes for that statue up there," speaking of Vulcan on Red Mountain to their south.

Killing time Cecil goads, "Robert here's a poet. He knows a Civil War poem—the whole danged thing." Cecil laughs a big one and slaps his thigh.

"Sure," Pape agrees, "like to hear it."

Robert responds, "What about Vulcan, Mr. Pape? My wife's uncle worked on that statue—one of a few survivors who did."

They still wait for their go ahead. They had been stationary a few minutes. They watched L&N's train go on north and their own train's flagman return with orders from a tower ahead. The crossing gate in front of them had been lifted, and they failed to see hindrance to their procession, but their signal still shone red. Robert goes back to his door to look down his left side of the train for hand signals. Cecil looks back down his side a little then turns around.

"Do it, Bob," Cecil urges. "Do the whole blessed poem. He does a bunch of them."

Robert likes limelight and thankful for any audience, and he's tempted but decides with a pleasant glance, "Not time nor place. Another opportunity awaits."

Cecil looks back and forth between his shotgun riders and signal light up ahead, "We got our signal." A signal right side of their track turns yellow. Again, their overhead buzzer sounds a two-tone signal from Mr. Sullivan, leaning and watching from an open Dutch door in a vestibule several cars back.

Pape agrees, "Yes, we do."

Robert looks ahead then up and down his side of train for hand signals, "That's us. All clear."

Cecil looks over his shoulder and ahead of the train at a green and yellow light signal at about 15 feet above and right of his track and clarifies, "All clear, proceed with caution, Fireman Gambrell—yard speed to the next signal." From his watch displayed in front of him, he announces, "2:01."

Pape looks straight ahead and makes a note on his pad.

Robert agrees, "All clear, proceed with caution, Engineer Love—yard speed," pulls his watch and confirms, "2:01." *Engineer Pyler and Fireman Alass receive orders. Forty-eight departs Tuscaloosa, two minutes late, consisting of engine, almost identical to Second 47's, combination coach-baggage car, coach, lounge-coach, three additional coaches, dining car, tavern-lounge-observation car, and 214 passengers.*

Cecil gives his whistle two short blasts signaling forward movement. He nudges his throttle a notch, and their long, sleek streamliner *The Crescent*, an anomaly, an L&N train with Southern engines running on Southern track as Second 47, eases forward—motion so smooth a passenger must look out and see scenery move to realize movement.

Late in life and nearing end of a decades long career, folk singer and songwriter John Prine wrote "Lonesome Friends of Science", a little more than four-minute song in which he claims to tackle, among other formidable subjects, a romantic escapade—Venus abandoning her Birmingham iron man, Vulcan—his nudity notwithstanding, one assumes—for Denver and Mars.

I heard it tonight, just a second ago, on PBS, recorded live at Saenger Theater, New Orleans.

4

Birmingham to Woodstock

Amtrak still runs a same route today and calls her *The Crescent,* but from 1941 until 1970, she was *The Southerner,* the Southern Railway's Southbound, #47, originating in New York City and going down the Seaboard to Philadelphia, Washington, DC, all the way to New Orleans. Its sister train, #48 began in New Orleans and went north making identical stops to New York City. In those days, the L & N operated *The Crescent* which followed a similar path but through Montgomery. On November 25, 1951, tracks on *The Crescent's* normal route experienced damage and trains diverted. The southbound *Crescent,* renamed this day as Second 47, came through Birmingham and followed *The Southerner,* # 47, toward Tuscaloosa and Meridian.

Road Foreman Pape steps back into a deafening engine room leaving Cecil and Robert alone in cab as Second 47 begins to move.

Embarking induces a creative urge in Uncle Cecil, one felt since inception by sage, author, songwriter, performer, and railroaders. He and Bob are rolling today in more ways than one. He begins to sing "Wabash Cannonball"—happy as can be.

> Listen to the jingle,
> the rumble, and the roar
> As she glides along the woodland,
> through the hills, and by the shore....

Pape returns before Cecil or his rendition of "Cannonball" gets going good. Cecil checks, "How we doin' up ahead, Bob?"

"Good to go, Cece. Lookin' good."

Cecil agrees, "Lookin' good."

The Wabash railroad existed in reality, but *The Cannonball,* music's mother of all trains, only in song, another casualty of romance and evasive fact. Cecil sings well and imagines *The Cannonball,* an easy thing to do.

Second 47 creeps through the Puzzle Switches at a few miles per hour, rocking back and forth like a cradle with squeaks and whines now accompanying constant rumble. They slide under World War I constructed viaducts: first, 24th Street; next, 22nd; and at 21st, Cecil informs, "This viaduct above us, Sam, is called 'Rainbow Bridge' after the Rainbow Division during the First World War."

Warehouses and office buildings, one to ten stories, line the rails as they approach two-storied L & N Station.

As promised, Cecil tries to school Pape on points of interest, "You know Union Station?"

Pape remains silent and involved on a paper in front of him.

Union Station, built in late 1800's, served all Birmingham's passenger service prior to Terminal Station. The L & N and a few minor players stayed, and Union Station became L & N Station. Cecil admires its structure on his right and figures it looks like his old childhood schoolhouse: dirty maroon brick and brown steep-sloping roofs, white painted gable trim and dormers, arched windows and doors, and weathervane. Robert heard someone call it Queen Anne Victorian architecture. Cecil likes to talk. They discuss most everything, this station included, on their runs together. It sits along 20th Street, Birmingham's north and south "Main Street", and faces Morris Avenue—brick and narrow, as if an alley, with warehouses on both sides dating back 75 years or more. Various spare L & N passenger rail cars sit empty and motionless around station yard.

The L & N provided some of the country's finest passenger trains and some came through old Union Station: *The South Wind* from Chicago to Miami; *The Hummingbird*, Cincinnati to New Orleans; *The Azalean; The Pan American; The Florida Arrow.* The L & N took lead in replacing old uncomfortable, rough-riding pre-war cars with silver, sleek, smooth riding streamliners—like jumping from a Model T into a Chrysler Imperial.

Pape continues looking down for most part, and Cecil moves on. Their grade increases as they take a slight rise and pass over 19th and 18th Streets. Everything looks akin to manufacturing or business: storage spaces, depositories, stockrooms, and idle boxcars. Signs read Moore-Handley, Fruit and Produce, Dixie Coal, Sears, and others simply say Coal, Ice, Auto, Iron and Steel.

Southern tracks make up two of about six main lines thru here. L & N, Seaboard, and Frisco (Saint Louis-San Francisco Railway Company) comprise others. Sidetracks on both sides complete a total rail reservation about sixteen tracks wide. Seventeenth, 16th, and 15th Streets dead end in both directions rather than transect an area of utmost importance and intense activity. University of Alabama's medical school functions a half dozen blocks south, on their left, as a few hospital buildings along with an extension center, little indication of an expansive four-year university and regional medical center to come in future decades.

Cecil, going over and looking down 17th Street on his right, tries again, "There's the Thomas Jefferson, Sam," referring to a luxury hotel near theater district. "That thing that looks like a radio tower on top actually is docking for blimps or some such deal."

They approach 14th Street interlocking and tower. An interlocking or interlocking plant has turnouts, sidetracks, and apparatus to safely control passing and crossing trains. This will be their last control tower open until Tuscaloosa. Mr. Love applies his brake, again evaluating its function, and they slow to a few miles per hour and train orders pass on a fork from a tower operator to Mr. Sullivan, conductor, in back. Fourteenth Street tower contains dozens of signal and switch controls, phones, telegraph, and old-fashioned manual signal devices. Here, the Frisco breaks north and west toward Fairfield furnaces and operations of U. S. Steel, TCI (Tennessee Coal, Iron, and Railroad Company), Republic Steel, and American Cast Iron and Pipe.

Robert thinks of Eugene, Gerry's father, who works up that way at Thomas Freight Yards. From there, trains go northwest toward Jasper, Tuscumbia, Memphis, and St. Louis.

In an opposite direction from 14th Street, the L& N mainline turns south toward Calera and Montgomery. For decades, this interlocking provided control of transport from Red Mountain ore mines at Spaulding, Oxmoor, Muscoda, and at one time, Irondale via a loop across and along the mountain below Vulcan's current perch. The Southern mainline continues straight thorough junction and siding, still on a vague, general path down valley.

All three can see a motionless freight's bright headlight a quarter mile south toward Green Springs. Passenger trains receive priority.

As they move farther southwest, Cecil pushes his throttle forward a notch, and they begin to cruise a little. Cecil says, "Fourteenth Street—2:06."

Robert repeats by his well-used Hamilton, "Fourteenth Street —2:06."

Engineer Pyler keeps 48 slow through a section of northeastern Tuscaloosa near Holt.

Pape's seen enough for now and takes opportunity to step sternward, "Going back to 2801, gents," speaking of their second engine just behind.

Cecil leans forward, "We gonna get 'er now, Bob. Ole 47 is out front a little, but we'll close a little by Tuscaloosa. You just watch."

Robert relaxes a bit in seat, folds arms on chest, and enjoys it all—every second a moving urban panorama seen from several times height of pedestrians and way above automobiles. He raises his hands to chest, fingertips touching and tapping, back in trance. He and Buster will finish his house, he and family will survive, we'll save some money. We'll make it. He wants railroad union work, deliberative challenges—a people job requiring linguistic and speaking abilities and a natural tendency to decipher circumstance and create results and solutions. He thinks himself capable, without question, even shrewd. He envisions wide travel and importance— connected to his rails yet far removed and away.

Second 47 consists of two engines, one mail car, a baggage-dormitory car, three coaches, one dining car, and seven sleeper cars, last of which includes lounge and observation area. Even in railroad's prime, she looks long, powerful, and fine.

They pick up some speed as Cecil blows for crossings through Birmingham's western area, each street's number lessening as they go. Before every crossing stands a reflective white sign with four horizontal black marks—one over another ordering a whistle response—a long, a long, a short, and a long. Cecil obliges each time by pulling his whistle cord, sometimes a little elongated or shortened a tad to be creative and others coming out harsh and emphatic at a vehicle or person taking a chance and risking it all to beat Cecil through a crossing. Sometimes someone just moves too "damned slow" through a danger zone for an engineer's liking—crews agree, folks are crazy.

In an era before widespread crossing signals and gates, most all seasoned engineers and firemen, Cecil, Robert, Pape included, have been on engines hitting vehicles and sometimes killing people —almost all trying to beat a train. Little an engineer or fireman or anyone can do.

From trains, as Robert and experienced riders know, everything by tracks in a city looks old. Train lines began it all, and earliest structures lie adjacent to rail's right-of-way. Jones Valley, as all original train routes, shows age.

Cecil adds, "It's a straight shot from here for a while," moving about 30 MPH. Cecil pulls hard on his whistle for Center Street. They make Elyton, where it all did, in fact, begin for these parts—a planned rail crossing and Elyton Land Company buying and selling land for a railroad reservation and development. On their left, on Center, they look almost into second story windows of 19th Century Elyton school. They continue westward. Cecil passes a speed limit sign allowing him to move it up another notch.

Cecil says, "Everything slick as owl—Powderly here in a minute."

In Pape's absence, Cecil again hums and sings to relax and break monotony, but more for himself. Robert, relying on some lip reading, can just make it out above engine,

> She came down from Birmingham
> one cold December day
> When she pulled into the station,
> you could hear all the people say
> She's a mighty tall and handsome,
> known quite well by all
> She came down from Birmingham
> on the Wabash Cannonball.

Cecil brakes a little for Powderly and dangerous crossings. He sounds his whistle as required and toots a few extra for cars, trucks, pedestrians, or even pets who, for whatever reasons, need reminding, Uncle Cecil Coming Through.

"Tell 'em, Uncle Cece'," Robert teases and sniggers.

Cece' winks, "They better know it."

Powderly epitomizes working class living with white, wooden, small one-stories, sometimes what rich call a shot house or worse. Miners grow strong, proud, black, and dirty and sore, but for them, as railroaders, it beats what they had. And, to hell with you if you failed to see it.

In Powderly, and places like it, a mining skeleton forms an embryonic center, and life swells around it.

Back in passenger cars, Conductor Sullivan keeps a steady, deliberate pace up and down aisles. His experience teaches him just how to stand to avoid losing balance and maybe tumbling as his train jolts and shifts. He seldom braces himself by grabbing over-head luggage racks for support as most do, "Tickets, please. Have your tickets ready." Southwest of Powderly he feels Engineer Love slow their train for a trestle north of Bessemer. Sullivan stops ticket collection, goes between cars, and again opens top section of a Dutch door to observe from right side of train.

Once over trestle, Cecil speeds up again to his 50 MPH limit for this section. Mr. Sullivan keeps his vestibule position, looking out for upcoming Woodward Crossing and Bessemer. Second 47's movement feels an effortless glide as if caressed and squeezed by Engineer Love's respective throttle and brake hand.

Road Foreman Pape retakes his middle seat in cab to Robert's right. "How's everything going, Bob?"

Robert nods, "Fine, fine, Sam. I think Cecil has it all under control—as is normal."

Seven miles out of Birmingham, their course remains due southwest and will for another 12 miles until they reach a couple of curves south of Kimbrel and Green Pond.

Woodward Crossing describes its own existence. A four-mile-long spur runs northwest, and a short line south off mainline, giving access to mines, quarries, furnaces, and mills.

Pape comments, "A lot of smoke."

Robert answers, "Always," and considers, today no different. He looks back out of far side of cab toward Fairfield, TCI, and U.S. Steel—burning and smoking.

Cecil slows her down further for a crossing north of Bessemer, largest town between Birmingham and Tuscaloosa. Cecil hits his whistle hard through here for crossings and activity around a Pullman car manufacturing plant, pipe and rolling mills, oil storage, junctions, and station.

Pape, restless and looking to fulfill his assigned duties, gets up again. He stretches, acts a little fidgety, "I'll think I'll go back and enjoy the view."

Cecil tries one last time, "Do you know what a beehive is, Pape?"

"Honey making"

"Right," Cecil chuckles and agrees, "they do, but in steel, a beehive is a sort of oven where they cook down coal to make coke to fuel all this. It looks like a beehive and Sloss has hundreds of them. Bessemer too. You can see them out this side sometimes."

"Interesting. I'll be in back."

"Nice day for a ride, Pape," Cecil likes his own voice as a way to stay awake and alert. "We got Burstall interlocking switch coming up."

Pape disappears to back, and Cecil quiets. Robert stands and from his hip pocket pulls his pipe, pops empty bowl on palm and contemplates his and Gerry's status after ten years or so of marriage —he studies to think how many. As a man who seldom doubts himself, he regrets to some degree their little spats of late and his performance over coffee this morning and, most of all, harsh words —it's not typical really, and he's unsure why it does happen at all. He figures, we've been bickering and both a little discontented or disconnected. It's marriage. He takes out an orange and silvery blue striped foil pouch of Sir Walter Raleigh from a cardboard box, size of a transistor radio. He also pulls out a matchbox, 2.5 x 1.5 inch, red and deep blue, inscribed, "Diamond, Since 1881". He gives his smoke a little thought and stuffs it all back in pocket. He'll smoke in Meridian. "I don't inhale anyway."

And he thinks of his station giftshop visit earlier and his saleslady—her legs—Dinah's legs. He likes that name—Great balls of fire. Great Scott.

Two thru tracks parallel Bessemer's station. A half dozen auxiliary tracks stockpile gondola cars of coal from surrounding coal fields and pig iron, named for iron ore's piglet shape after cooling. Bulkhead and flat cars store lumber and plywood from down south.

Fresh pulp and wood chips look ready for travel to paper mill in Tuscaloosa. Limestone fills hopper cars, pale and washed out, white and gray.

Cecil, a little downhome in Pape's absence, "You know, that danged paper mill in 'Loosa shore does stink, dudn't it, Bob—like kraut. But a lot of folks say it smells like bread and butter."

"I know it," Robert laughs and checks time. "In a minute, Burstall approaches, and you can let her go, Uncle Cece."

Cecil cuts his eyes, "Reckon so."

Robert continues, "Indeed, time is of the essence, is it not. 2:16."

Forty-eight winds among knolls and crooks in eastern Tuscaloosa County, her pace slow and crew quiet. They chug due east, seven miles out of Cottondale, passing antiquated cotton mills. Engineer Pyler, two days short of his 69th birthday, makes up time as he can, considering topography. He dresses work casual as most but in all dark cotton, charcoal, long sleeves, black work boots and railroad cap with stitched orange caboose on front. A couple of months before, he completed 44 years as a Southern engineer. His hatless fireman, C. R. Alass, turned 35 two weeks prior and has 14 years seniority. Unlike Second 47, chatter lags as they ease through Coaling, north of Tuscaloosa. Pyler and Alass check their Hamilton's, they're still a little late. Track like this makes closing time difficult. Most trains catch up north of Woodstock.

"What y'all up to?" Baggageman E. B. Walters sticks his head into Second 47's cab from rear, and steps in—tall, lanky, young with bowl shaped, mussed hair, innocent face, and a plain crushed ball cap of yellow-flecked garnet.

"Come on in, E. B., just reciting poetry, singing—reflecting," Robert jests and feels a little lost in himself. He loves humor and words and thought but at one moment in time, here and now, he feels far removed from Sir Walter Raleigh, Shakespeare, history, and poets. He can't get his morning cup of coffee, 'fee-'fee, out of his mind either and how it ran over.

"How's that now?"

"Just talking, E. B., and moving on." Robert has retaken his seat on left side of train. "Have a seat. You leave Road Foreman Pape back there?"

Crew, baggagemen included, sometimes ride in a trailing unit, second engine, when a train has one, to observe. From a back facing unit, an observer in rural areas looks along his train as it bends and twists, left and right and up and down among hills, valley, and streams.

E. B. continues to stand. "That's just it. I come up just to shoot the bull a little, you know. Ole Sam, that guy, came back there, so I come up here. Know what I mean? Y'all want a sandwich? I got some baloney back there and some mayonnaise. Got some crackers too."

Cecil brakes a bit for Burstall, bumping down—one notch, two notch, three notch, four.

"Everything okay, Mr. Love?"

Cecil fails to respond but Robert answers, "Cecil's good, E. B. He's got food, he's fine."

E. B. says, "Actually, I'd rather shoot a little bull, but I'd better get back, if y'all ain't gonna ask me to stay and have no sandwich with y'all." He grins, and conversation disappears. "We're at Burstall. See y'all."

Cecil gets serious, citing orders, "Okay, Bob, from here at Burstall interlocking on, we are on CTC all the way to Tuscaloosa."

Robert nods, "Correct."

Burstall consists of a tower, small switches and sidetrack, and a main junction where Southern's mainline to and from Selma and Mobile connects with its Birmingham-New Orleans route. As of

October 10, centralized traffic control (CTC) rules the single line going southwest to Tuscaloosa, a first for Alabama. Crews found their new system different but preferable to traditional superiority of trains systems in which a trains class or timetable or train order decides priority in passing and intersecting. Train signals at track-side take precedence and guide trains, and in some places, an automatic train-stop system (ATS) began to initiate brake application when a train passed a restrictive speed signal. Robert and Cecil, as all crews, received proper training and qualifying examinations. A popular benefit of ATS allows trains to hit 80 when track condition allows.

Cecil speeds her up—notch at a time, smooth and gentle but definite. This was as straight and ideal as track gets for these trains. Easy grades lie ahead, traffic signal green.

Cecil hammers up and glances over, taking no prisoners, Brother Gambrell. "Highball."

Robert stares at him, make hay while sun shines, Brother Love. "Highball."

Second 47's twin engines feel like they tilt back as Cecil's left hand moves its powerful throttle forward and faster, and his fireman, conductor, and passengers lean rearward with her.

Trees, close to railroad's right-of-way on each side, appear a blur and reflections and shadows flash into windows of engines and rail cars as if pulsating strobes, faster every time. Cecil edges her up a notch. Highball is right.

Highball lingers as simple, traditional railroad jargon. In old days, before electrical signals at trackside, people moved a ball up and down to display orders to an oncoming train. A high ball meant go, all clear, full speed ahead, ball-a-jack.

Robert reiterates in a muffled whisper as he bends forward in seat and touches left fingers to forehead, as if a thinker, "Highball, Cece."

Eighty miles per hour equates express land travel in most years. In 1951, it felt like flying. Trains became so much smoother post-war.

Cecil blows two longs-a short-and a long for a small country road crossing, and they're through it and gone.

Trees by train come and go in insufficient time for focusing. Robert gazes through them at an abandoned field of straw-yellow orchard and Johnson grasses leading to a faded red, gambrel-roofed barn with open doors and a three-wheeled, rotten-wood wagon out front. A second or two later, it's all gone—in their past.

Cecil contends as if someone listening, "'It's the Orange Blossom Special bringin' my baby back.' Play that fiddle, boy."

Road Foreman Pape returns to cab and his middle seat, Robert to his left.

Robert asks, "Did you see E. B. Walters, the baggageman, back there, Sam?" He evaluates Pape as he does everyone and everything in short time.

"Yep. He's making sandwiches."

Cecil blows as Second 47 rambles through McCalla. They face hamlets from here to Tuscaloosa: Kimbrel, Green Pond, Woodstock, Vance, Coaling. A single track, starting at Burstall, stretches through countryside in front of them, little reason to slow.

Late November in these small hills means late fall colors as Robert saw this morning on Ruffner Mountain and at home: scarlet red, burnt orange, creamy yellow and browns. Blue sky governs above, save for a three-quarter waning white moon, up and behind them, already visible in dry sky. In front and right, to their southwest, a near four weeks-shy of solstice sun comes right down track at them. Thickets of stunted sweet gum, briars, poison ivy, honey locust, privet, trumpeter vines and spindly pines form a wall, a buffer along railroad right-of-way.

They're rockin' 'n' rollin'.

Rifle season for deer begins around Thanksgiving in Alabama, and every few miles a weekend hunter or two in orange safety cap and vest walks crossties to a new location to enter adjacent woods. Sometimes they pause on track to observe and wait. As Second 47 approaches, they take refuge behind brush and brambles and sometime raise a hand hello. They probably wonder what's going on since First 47 zoomed by only ten minutes prior.

"They're out today, gentlemen," Cecil announces. Robert and Pape seem content to observe.

Deer travel when hunted, seeking cover, spooked by gun shots, flushed by stalkers, and run by dogs. They too utilize railroad's right-of-way's edge cover and easy movement and footing, and they come for continuous rows of wild grass between track and along hedge rows so close to forests and fields. They flourish in a variety of cover and food, as do possum, raccoons, skunk, ground hogs, squirrel, rabbits, and boar. Crows and starlings land and forage along tracks. Sometimes, a startled eagle, hawk, or owl soars with expansive, majestic wings spread wide. Railroad crews become accustomed to hitting wildlife, especially deer at night. In day, much as their human counterparts, animals exercise poor judgment and underestimate speed of oncoming disaster, at night, they blind in unforgiving headlight beam.

"We just missed one," Cecil acknowledges of a doe. "Not sure if we did or not."

Pape coughs, "Why heck, yeah."

Robert prolongs his stare out into coal country—Cecil usually mentions it in this section. Football flashes through Robert's mind —Auburn and Alabama on Saturday in Birmingham—he'll usher as he does most Legion Field games.

Cecil obliges, "Coal Country along here."

A house or two, from time to time, sit on hillside and in clearing, snug and cozy, and away from track. Most exhibit white wood and slate colored shingle roofs with porch and swing, rocker, lawn chair, or all three. Some keep junk and old tires. Others stay as neat as a churchyard. Sunday means family day in the country, kids play in front, and old and young, filled with dinner and fellowship, wave.

As Cecil does on occasion, he toots an extra-short, barely audible greeting and looks to Pape.

A pond by a wooded spot catches Robert's eye and kindles household examination, something saved for sporadic occasion. He calculates his youngest son to be six—no, maybe five—and loves to fish. Frank Sparks, who he just saw back at station, has mentioned taking a father and son trip up on Elk River in North Alabama, and Robert makes mental note to accept invitation. Sparks likes to tie up boat under Shoal Creek Bridge, just upstream from Tennessee River and fish all night under a lantern for stripes, crappie, cat', what-have-you. Of course, Sparks likes a "wee sip" from a brown bag sometimes too—good way to go. And let's see, his oldest, based on younger's age, must be eight and a bigtime railroader already. Sometime when he fires with Windy Martin, eldest of local engineers, they might load that young boy on engine with them for train ride of his life to Chattanooga or Meridian.

Cecil blows again at a hobo looking character along track just above Kimbrel. This time, his whistle screams two complete, emphatic shorts. As with houses, pedestrians, vehicles, hunters, animals, alike, his whistle says hello or notes acknowledgement, but he intends to remind all to stay off our track, out of our way, beware, once again, we are coming through—now, today, tomorrow, and beyond.

He blows whistle crossing code again for a secondary road. Once across, he affirms looking at next signal high on track's right, "Kimbrel, green."

Robert confirms, "All green, Kimbrel."

A mail station once existed beside crossing, but trains saw Kimbrel as a signal just south of a dying little community. A southbound knew it as their first curve in about 12 miles. Cecil brakes and slows to 65, and into curve they go.

Robert pulls his watch—2:23. *Northbound 48 parallels U. S. Highway 11 through and out of Vance, a former trading post, along Tuscaloosa and Bibb County line. Engineer Pyler keeps his 70 miles per hour speed constant, cruising a northeastern bearing. Talk stays almost nonexistent.*

Cecil perseveres in attempted conversation, his partners lulled. "That sun's going be a problem later on as it gets down more. Bright enough as it is." He throttles back up again as they come out of curves and barrel southwest.

They pass well managed loblolly pine close to train—fast growth pulpwood, four to nine-inch diameter, and well-thinned straight saw timber, ten inches and above—all showing shiny, yellow-green needled crowns—evergreen, persistent, and pretty in oncoming winter.

Things become and remain quiet. Miles vanish.

Every move of Cecil's hands and speedometer attract attention. Cecil keeps things in line as his good reputation avows.

Robert recalls training, for every doubling of velocity, force required to stop quadruples.

Conductor Sullivan got busy after Burstall, gobbling up tickets in his last coach and lacks only a few more before new passengers load in Tuscaloosa.

Between Kimbrel and Green Pond, Cecil yanks his whistle cord for a lane—too small, rural, and backwoods for maps.

Pape asks, "Who owns all this timber?"

Robert and Cecil reply about same time, "Belcher." Robert adds, "Practically all of it." Robert and his brothers know people who sawmill in Bibb County. Belcher became more than a southern timber baron. As with Pullman in Illinois with rail cars, Peabody in Kentucky with coal, and Drummond, a coal dynasty an hour or so north, magnates grow larger than life. Workers call boss land-lord, financier, merchant, overlord, governor, sometimes spiritual-ist. Life ain't always fair, no one said it was. Through this section, Robert and Cecil sometimes discuss "Sixteen Tons", a song Cecil sings. Unsure who first sang it or wrote it, they love it, a coal miner song about working all day, providing coal, but just getting older and deeper in debt. Saint Peter calls yet a worker can't go—he owes his soul to the company store. Merle Travis wrote it, and Tennessee Ernie Ford, for one, recorded it later.

After deserved silence, Robert checks, "How we doing, Cecil?"

"I got 2:30 and on time, Bob."

Highballing southbounds reduce speed shy of Green Pond crossing before throttling up for increasing grade.

In Car 4, Conductor Sullivan always keeps two seats facing each other as a makeshift office, right side on forward end of car. All ticketing complete, he counts receipts, stubs, monies, and plans for Tuscaloosa's stop. Most of all, this section of track always allows time to tip back his hat, straighten in his seat, breath deep, gaze out, and catch his bearings.

Robert checks up on Cecil's declaration, "Yep, 2:30." *Forty-eight has been moving northward at controlled speed since a red over yellow signal north of Vance. At two thirty, they come head-to-head with First 47 about 40 feet in front of them, stopped on the mainline at a switch just south of Woodstock—Woodstock south switch. As planned by a dis-patcher in Birmingham, 48 northbound moves over south switch, flexing as a snake, section by section onto a sidetrack—car by car until it clears mainline. First 47, stopped at Woodstock south, blows "SIGNALS" as a re-minder and indicator to 48: Another train, Second 47, follows behind. With*

48 clear south switch and mainline, motionless First 47 gets a green signal to proceed on southwestward toward Tuscaloosa. Everything functions as clockwork.

After 48 northbound clears Woodstock's south switch, a track signal, red over yellow, instructs Pyler and Alass to proceed down sidetrack at yard speed to next signal just before Woodstock north switch where sidetrack rejoins mainline.

From northeast, Cecil, Robert, and Pape roar into Green Pond. Two longs, a short, a long blare for Green Pond's crossing—Cecil's warning to all.

"Thanks to you gentlemen for your hospitality today," Pape gives a slight and quick index finger informal salute. "You're most amiable." He repositions in middle chair. They all feel relaxed for a smooth section of trip and warm autumn sun. Passengers in rear feel it too, everyone sits back.

"I hear you, Sam," Cecil acknowledges. Robert nods polite recognition.

Cecil glances at time in front of him—2:32. *Engineer Pyler continues to move 48 along sidetrack toward his next signal and Woodstock north switch, now less than 1.62 miles ahead. Forty-eight's conductor opens a Dutch door top section and stands in a vestibule on Car 4 to observe. He finds a gorgeous day to absorb railroading at its best. They pass a small, quaint, commonplace, almost forgotten station with typical identification on each end—Woodstock. Farther back, 48's Flagman, takes a similar position on 48's last coach, Car 6.*

Engineer Pyler turns his head to Fireman Alass, "I wonder if we are going to get away for Second 47." Alass remains silent.

Green Pond exists as another almost invisible unincorporated community on Second 47's trip. Through a country road crossing, they face Signal 1699's green glow. Cecil slows a notch or so as customary, and Pape thumbs timetables, orders, and forms, as if passing time.

They all look up a long steady incline of over a mile, maybe mile and a quarter, to where track doglegs—leans right and bends into Woodstock.

"All clear on 1699," from behind throttle.

"All clear," Robert's confirmation. As he often does, he stretches his neck a little, fudging right from his seat to make out Cecil's speedometer.

Pape places papers in travel bag where he keeps best laid plans.

They proceed onward and upward. Crew remains seated and silent. At crest of hill, their engine levels and curves more westward looking into sunlight and Woodstock.

Middle seat sits highest, Pape jumps up first, My God, he's on the mainline.

5

Bad News Travels Like Wildfire

Down South they call dinner any meal between breakfast and bedtime snack. Gerry and kids ate plenty by mid-afternoon at Grandma and Grandpa's.

Emma Bueteker Goodyear, Gerry's adoptive mother, lives good as good as good gets—to reuse and reword a phrase. Of Swiss descent, her southern and German style cooking excels. She lies down for a nap and Grandpa, Eugene, on such an ideal afternoon, returns to his front porch where Robert last saw him. Gerry helps clean Emma's kitchen, and kids watch Grandpa's 16-inch Philco TV on mahogany stand. Grandpa and grandkids love his new TV. As most everyone in 1951, they rather watch an odd, newfangled, black and white screened contraption than do anything else.

In middle bedroom, Emma gets up from her single bed. She stands tall, a couple inches or so under six feet, her bones large but graceful. She harbors only goodwill and loves without flaunting or pretext. Humility rules her being, people know her as unpretentious.

She starts to wash her face and hands for evening service. Her face looks rounded, skin swarthy, hair natural and short, and her eyes twinkle and glimmer. Conservative and fashionable for her time, born in 1888, she wears bonnets and long and full high bust lined pleated dresses, plain hose and corsets. Evening approaching, she moves past her grandkids toward kitchen and Gerry.

On his front porch, still seated and comfortable, Eugene checks Hamilton—4:16. In less than an hour, this time of year, darkness falls. Elongating shadows engulf his lawn and sidewalk. His willow oak rattles in a slight breeze.

His screen door swings open, "Daddy, in few minutes, we'll have turkey sandwiches and some of Mama's vinegary, warm German potato salad you love so much. She'll be going to church, and the kids and I'll be heading home." Eugene listens, and Gerry examines him a moment, knows he heard, and smiles at his lack of response. She buzzes back inside—*juning* again.

Up 55th comes Mr. Street, given name unknown to everyone. Grandpa calls him Deac'.

He walks with his feet out, a penguin, in soft black loafers and dumpy, cuffed, beltless pants of faded periwinkle and black checks. His V-neck tee shirt's tail, around a bellied waistline, on any day, remains half in and half out. He wears tin looking, narrow rimmed, rectangular bifocals. His wet cigar stub dangles from mouth.

"Hello, Deac'!" Eugene welcomes from afar.

Mr. Street tramps sidewalk, his loose shoes scuffling, still a house or so away. He disregards any distraction. Few, if any, know Mr. Street's vocation. Someone might have referred to him as machinist, but where remains another question. He may care for an invalid wife—depending on to whom you listen. Chances are scuttlebutt has it wrong.

Mr. Street halts where Robert stood earlier, an exact spot where everyone stands, as if actors hitting their mark—the Goodyear's talking point—where their little concrete walk meets big world.

"How you doin' Deac'?" Eugene asks in a tone of sincere fondness and regard for his friend, something he saved for some.

Deac' pulls out his gnawed, tar colored cigar butt and removes his straw, dented Fedora. He shakes all over. His bottom lip hangs bulbous, red, indeed lifeless, and long, one side of his face to other, and moves in slight, unsteady, almost indiscernible jaw jerks, as if partly paralyzed, creating imprecise pronunciation and broken enunciation. "Hello, 'Gene."

"Missed you Saturday," Eugene refers to their regular card or game day—everything from Canasta to Dominoes to Checkers to Chinese Checkers to Go Fish. They play on a card table behind where Eugene sits, in a front bedroom, and they argue over every disagreement. If any money changes hands, Emma doesn't know it. But, fingers point, heads shake, threats and wars wage, canes wave, names call, and friendships diminish or disappear until Saturday or next meeting in between. They missed yesterday due to holiday weekend.

Without beating around bush, "Say, 'Gene, I was listening on the radio, and they said something about a train wreck. Did you hear that?"

"No." Eugene comes across gruff when required, a man of few words and faces.

Mr. Street pauses several seconds. "Well, they said it was between here and Tuscaloosa—two passenger trains. And, you know, I thought I better tell 'Gene—'cause I know you work in Thomas Yard and you know some people. That's all. I didn't hear much."

He places Fedora back on, returns a little residual piece of cigar to mouth, chews and rotates it.

"Well, I'm glad you did, Deac'. I'm glad you did."

"Have you been watchin' today, 'Gene? I know you got TV."

"No, but hell, can't watch anything around here lately, Deac'. Those kids—"

Mr. Street figures, "No, guess you can't."

"I appreciate you telling me, 'Deac." Eugene sits motionless for a moment. "Think I'll go inside."

Mr. Street turns to walk home, "Just thought—better let 'Gene know. See you Saturday."

Eugene remains seated a few minutes. His street, a few weeks from winter, looks lonely and deserted except for Deac' plodding home. In summer, teens ride bikes up and down this time of day, selling popsicles from metal ice boxes mounted on front of bicycles —for a few cents. In late autumn, people go in earlier, leaves detach and settle, weather fronts begin moving through, and winds blow.

Eugene stands, feeling stiff and slow. He picks up a horsehead cane, leaning against his chair. He uses it on off days, working on his feet takes a toll. He ambles inside, through his living room, stopping to change televisions channels. His grandkids love Grandpa, his sternness, and they know to avoid arguing. Children like good, fair, well thought out, consistent discipline. He turns a knob, right and below his screen, "We need to watch this," and he cusses over static and poor reception and yanks rabbit ears in all directions— impatient and cranky. He tells his grandboys, "Now, leave it there— on that channel. That channel. Don't move it, and don't change it." And they don't, they retreat to another room.

Gerry enters from kitchen, "You ready to eat, Daddy? I'll get that," and starts to assist though she knows zero about new technology. Adjusting and controlling TV will become simple one day, much less so now.

"No, you come in here," and he starts back, cane still in hand, past dining room and through his bedroom's open door.

She walks past him and jostles his arm as if to liven him, "Let me get these sandwiches out to the kids, Mama's leaving for church. Be there—momento."

Eugene waits in his bedroom, looking from a lone window over tranquil side yard toward their neighbor's white frame and wine roofed house disappearing in fast falling darkness.

Their Goodyear home, as basic inside as out in structure, houses deep, endless, and unquestionable love, trust, and giving. Gerry's childhood home, as her person, harbors personal warmth and champions positivity.

Their house consists of three bedrooms, living room, kitchen and bath. For heat, two fireplaces and a stove remain unused for years, a 3x5 metal grated gas floor furnace between living and dining rooms roasts you if you stand on or near it too long. Ceilings rise high—10 feet or better—with passages filled, in most part, by open doors and transoms. Functionality prevails, a sign of times and personalities.

Grandpa takes his seat on his standard feather bed, looking back into his house at window and all-important radio, and at his 45 Colt pistol, long barreled, pearl handled, covered with white sleeveless tee shirt, and stuck in a nightstand magazine holder as holster. He has his rocker nearby, and a nightshirt and handkerchief hang on it. He can reach his lifelines and his tobacco, a few cigars, pipe, roll your own cigarettes, and out of sight from Emma, a hidden bottle for a nip or two of what she calls his snake medicine.

Eugene's RCA tabletop radio resembles a big reddish brown plastic shoebox. When on, a bright orange "Power On" light burns in front, dominating and glaring. Tubes, illuminated within, glow yellow from its open back and through speaker holes in front. He listened to everything before TV and still likes his baseball. Radio remains important to Eugene, born in 1884, it defines his era.

But today—Eugene seeks news. He twists and turns his tuner knob for results or anything sounding local. He keeps one ear open for anything on his TV, volume loud in his living room.

"Okay, Daddy, what is it?" Gerry comes from kitchen, "And, why in the world are that TV and radio so loud?" Gerry goes to turn TV down.

Eugene stands, "No, stay here and listen," aiming his finger at his radio. He turns it up for her and hurries, as he seldom does, to his living room with his little black book in his cane hand.

"What is the matter with you, Daddy?"

He pivots to face her on his way out and uses his hand to emphasize. "Just stay here and listen like I told you. Just do what I tell you."

Gerry returns his gaze as if asking, what in Halifax—Emma's euphemism for hell.

In his living room, Eugene delves into his little black book and calls a number on their house phone—party line being open. Gerry remains oblivious to whom or why. She barely hears her daddy with radio and television volume peaking. He talks on a big heavy receiver of a black rotary phone, more like rubber than plastic. What he says remains mystery, but she hears him hang up.

Gerry stands by end of her father's bed, where he left her, until he returns, as serious as before or more so. She asks again, "What is going on?"

"I don't want to say anything for sure, or be wrong, or sound a false alarm, until I'm sure, and I'm still not—not exactly, but I better—"

"Better what? Say anything about what?" She drops to his bed, listening, Eugene still standing.

"Well, 'Deac said something a minute a go—" and her father, a succinct man of frankness and certainty, pauses—unsure, tentative, and reticent.

"What's wrong?" Gerry knows this man, something is wrong, bad wrong.

"I don't know. I just don't know much for sure, but I called over at the telegraph office—at the yard, and there's been a wreck," and stops for air.

"What kind of wreck?"

"Just listen, and don't—"

From there on, everything becomes fuzzy in her mind, it all happens fast. She remembers little pieces for a while.

She remembers a news announcement on radio and her father saying Robert's brother is coming.

Emma, unaware or unaffected or unbeaten and unconquered, walks from their porch toward church, a couple of blocks away.

Grandpa starts to follow, to tell her what happened, but reverses before reaching his door.

More wreck information may be a while. News stories develop over time. Details—in that era—may come in hours, days, weeks, months, or more, if at all. For Gerry, everything seems a blank, a blackboard without writing.

Gerry stands beside him without a word, as many times before, for long minutes until necessity overcomes dissociation, "Well, I have to do something. I'll call Lucille and C. W. or Frank Sparks." Both men rested or slept, having just come in earlier from their late arriving Chattanooga run but their phones began buzzing. Lucille, Gerry's lifelong friend, says several people have called and mentioned a wreck somewhere, but she let C. W. sleep. She'd wake him and have him call back as soon he knows more. She says her husband and Sparks saw Robert at the station when they came in and he was going out." Gerry called Sparks several times but got only busy signals.

Her mind becomes more unclear, "Maybe, I should call Charles and Brad," referring to Robert's brothers.

Eugene replies, "Charles is on his way. He was going to church at East Lake Methodist, but he's coming here. He called Brad."

"I'll call Catherine Edge," a childhood friend a half block away.

"She doesn't know anything about all this, Geraldine, just wait for C. W. Cottrell or Sparks to call back. They'll know more than anybody and if it's Robert's train or what's happened. We're not sure. We're just going by radio and TV, and they don't know anything."

Eugene and Geraldine sit together, side by side, in a dark room, sun has set. Kids finish eating and go back to playing. They want to watch more TV, some other night. They wonder about going home as planned, maybe later. They start to complain of boredom, find something to do.

Emma returns long before Sunday night prayer meeting got going good. She knows of trouble but avoids asking. She works in her kitchen, putting food away, scrubbing, and tidying. Details surface soon enough, they always do.

C. W. calls back. "Without a doubt, Gerry, it is Robert's train. I talked to a telegraph operator, a tower man, a trainmaster, and the Call Boy, but that's all I know. It looks like a bad situation." Yet, for soul of him, he cannot find anyone who knows what happened or why or wants to say anything or make any comment on conditions regarding status of passengers or even crews or anything specific.

Gerry escapes to her childhood porch, its coolness and darkness. She hops up on a wooden three-seater swing and starts back and forth, gazing down 55th, past Mr. Street's, over stadium hedges, across elementary and high school campuses, toward Woodlawn Baptist and Methodist steeples. She sat here often as a child, swinging and legs kicking. She hears a freight whistle, north of Woodlawn Hill, passing Gate City and Irondale, heading for Chattanooga. Gerry rubs her hands on her face, forehead, and eyes. "Damn."

Gerry waits for Charles's arrival, uncertain of what lies ahead. Her daddy keeps up with any news and calls. In a few minutes, C. W. calls back to ask if they're sure there isn't something he can do. He'll let them know if he hears anything else at all. He's been calling the Southern offices, but lines remain busy. He talked to Sparks and Red Duncan, and they all do the same. If there is anything to be known up and down a railroad line, these men know it.

Gerry hears Eugene, her dear daddy inside, still calling the railroad, and she gets up and begins walking a route she knows well: across porch, down three steps, up the Goodyear's walk, over where Robert stood this morning, and down 55th, and past Mr. Street's. How many times Gerry walked this way in life exceeds calculation—to school, church, store, theater, streetcar line, 5 & 10, soda fountain, post office, and Lucille's. Things grow so quiet after dark, always have, but she knows her sidewalk well, like the back of her hand. Everything always looks pitch black other side of fence hedges—dividing football field, stadium, schools, and churches from home.

Only a little more than a half block from the Goodyear's, Gerry goes left on Church Street, more of an alley by Woodlawn Baptist Church, site of her baptism as an infant. She raises her head to her church's steeple—supplicating, petitioning, imploring. Gaping up, she begs, help poor Robert. At her back, several dozen yards away, First Avenue carries light traffic on Sunday night. She glances to where a car hit Eugene, her brother by adoption, knocked him down, busted his head as if a watermelon on a streetcar rail. Inside, church service ends, and congregation disbands.

Gerry hustles at a fast clip along First Avenue, past hardware, drug store, dinette, and grocery. Back at corner of 55th, she looks across First at Woodlawn Theater where she saw Gone with the Wind—Rhett informing Scarlet, "Frankly, dear, I don't give a damn."

Gerry envisions it all again: a typical theater in its day but so warm and friendly, a haven. She absconded often, almost weekly—before TV days. She can see herself and friends, in 1930 or so, running up through parked bicycles to a glass ticket box, buying a pass for a nickel, then sprinting through a turnstile, pushing open multiple black doors, and racing to hard wooden seats—and imaginations ran wild.

Gerry spins and gazes up again—this time at Woodlawn Methodist's bell tower. Help Robert and help all of them.

She hurries, sure daddy wonders her whereabouts. Crossing Georgia Road, she steps back on curb to avoid an oncoming vehicle. Charles pulls up in a white '49 Chevy, big, sporty, waxed, and cool—four in floor. She looks at its long sloping fastback.

"Hey, lady, need a ride with a fine gentleman?"

Charles has her home, a couple of blocks at most, in seconds.

Charles Edward. Gambrell, 25, Robert's youngest brother, fresh out of school and coming off honeymooning, gained employment as an accountant for TCI, a large steel manufacturer with local prominence. Gerry and everyone consider him most even tempered, consistent, and positive of three brothers.

Eugene knows little more than when Gerry left to go wandering. Good information coming out of Woodstock remains limited and muddled and slow.

"Daddy, we're going to Brad's in West End and then on down."

Charles stands beside her on porch. "Yes, sir, Mr. Goodyear, I talked to the sheriff's office here in Birmingham—with mixed results. He thinks there's an information or emergency center or something set up down there to help people find out what's going on."

Gerry adds, "We can do better when we get down there."

Eugene updates, "C. W. Cottrell called back. He said they were taking injured to Bessemer or Tuscaloosa or somewhere. I tried to call the railroad over at the yards and downtown at the office—no answers and busy or out of service signals."

Charles concurs, "All the phone lines are overloaded, fouled up and tied up everywhere."

"It'll be okay," as she neglects her hair and face and leaves purse behind. Eugene hands her a sweater as she goes out. "We'll be back. Robert can come back with us in Charles's car. There's more room than in our truck. Robert will need a ride somewhere. We'll be home—back here—in a couple of hours or so."

Her father starts to refute, "Geraldine—" but lets it drop. He follows her out to his porch and shakes Charles's hand. She takes Charles's arm as they descend steps, and he leads to his Chevy. They cruise away, as Robert did earlier, up to next intersection for U-turn and hum by. Eugene watches Charles's small, round taillights —mounted on long, slanted trunk—fade away. Eugene looks to his Hamilton—7:32. He feels as grim as he looks, sitting alone again on his porch, temperature dropping in dry air. He takes it all in best he can—for better or worse—unpleasant as can be.

6

Good News Travels Slow

I like to see it lap the miles—
And lick the valleys up—
And stop to feed itself at tanks—
And then prodigious step
—Emily Dickinson, #585

One song we sang in shower back then and played some on guitar—Rock Island Line—had a line explaining it's all right for a northbound train to leave on a southbound track—but he won't be back. They say Lead Belly wrote it—a really old, musty and rusty rail song—or he receives credit. It goes way back. We were just kids and didn't really care who or why.

Before and since, folks love to call Woodstock a peaceful, sleepy little railroad siding for coal, ore, cotton, and lumber. Two enormous antebellum homes show minimal life. A Gothic 19th

Century United Methodist Church renews twice a week for meeting. In a general store, outdated merchandise carries a film of charcoal colored, months old dust, and on countertop, a handwritten message—Ring for Service—on a taped-on index card hangs loose from a silver little bell nonfunctional for months and everyone, dozing store clerk included, fails to notice.

On Sunday afternoon, all hell broke loose. Five and a half hours later, at 8 PM, Second 47's and 48's engines still smoke. Emergency workers and rescue teams set up spotlights, loudspeakers, and cranes to work in darkness. Every piece of metal must be turned, in case a survivor or body part ended up underneath. Ambulances, fire trucks, and police cars come and go. An entire hollow of woods and fields fills with people, equipment, and intensity.

A fellow sitting on his mother's porch after dinner sees some of it through rail right-of-way pines. A couple of strollers, walking and facing away, down by station and store, maybe a quarter mile away, hear it and turn around seconds later. One young man, who everyone calls "The Wind", says he watched every bit of it, but refuses to make an official statement until over a half century later. For decades, he describes details to locals at every opportunity— saying it reminded him of war—as if a giant bomb went off. Forty-eight's massive engine shot backwards, against its will, for 50 to 60 feet. Its third car, a loaded Colored coach, telescoped. Second 47's two engines halted and crumpled. Its baggage car went off a ravine into a mining spur track passing beneath mainline, and numerous cars jumped track. And I'll tell you, he exclaims, the whole danged place went crazier than a loon. He picnicked on the Methodist church lawn, eating a baloney sandwich and pork skins. Ten minutes after a massive bang, he confides, a whole world of commotion and confusion descended on us, Friends.

Gerry and Charles seek news, good or bad. From the Goodyear's in Woodlawn, in Charles's car, they follow Gerry and Robert's route of almost 12 hours before, over viaduct by Sloss furnaces, and through downtown heading west. They stop at a house in West End, close to Arlington Home, an Antebellum home constructed decades before Birmingham existed.

Brad, Henry Bradford Gambrell, middle brother runs out and jumps in, Gerry in middle. As they go, they cross rail tracks several times where Cecil, Robert, and Pape blew through hours earlier.

Gerry thinks Brad shares his brothers' stature, medium build and height. His skin, as his brothers', with slight ruddiness and tint, fits well against proportioned facial bones—snug and tight. His eyes, like Robert's, smaller than Charles's, dart. He always smiles in reserved silence, he has a smooth, charming Frenchman look. Charles's face and eyes, more rounded, exude openness, familiarity, and spirituality. Robert and Brad possess equal charm, but sacred cores lie deeper, more removed and difficult to tap.

Their pilgrimage proceeds south. Gerry knows Brad, even better than Charles, going back to her first meeting Robert in Woodlawn Highlands and from Silver Slipper dancing days, something Charles avoided. She feels comfortable with men of calm integrity, honesty, and judgment.

Charles asks, "How's it going at U.S. Steel, H.B? You still keeping corporation afloat and solvent?"

Brad does his feint, endearing grin and looks down shaking head, "Mercy." He began work a couple of years before. At 30, he's on a fast track up or, at least, an inviting stairway to upper management. Both men, for most, educated themselves—paid their way through school. As Robert's little brothers, they survived near poverty youth, Depression, and World War II combat.

Charles plans, "We'll stop at Bessemer General. I talked to some public relations person at the Southern Office in Birmingham. He didn't know much."

Brad answers, "Naturally," still pleasant. Patience runs low for everyone.

"He referred me to the Bibb County or Tuscaloosa County Sheriff's office—"

Brad adds, "Woodstock is in Bibb."

Charles goes on, "Yep. So, I tried and mostly got busy signals and phone service unavailability messages. The only thing I did find out from anybody was that there's some temporary disaster infor-mation centers set up. One's at a store called Mayfield's just west of Woodstock on Highway 5 or 11. The railroad has people there too, to help hopefully. People are being taken to Bessemer General or Druid City Hospital in Tuscaloosa."

"Any idea how many or who?" Brad asks.

Charles shakes his head.

"And I wonder what they do with people who are aren't hurt bad. I mean everyone's not injured badly, I guess." Brad thinks a second. "And, how do you know if someone's—?" He lets it drop off—incomplete. After a few seconds, "Really hurt."

"Don't know, H. B."

"Me either, 'Phe." Brad and others call Charles 'Phe, short for Apostrophe, he being most black headed, a bit small, short, and as youngest, bringing up rear. "Are you okay, Gerry?"

"I am, Brad," keeping chin up, "and thank ya'll for this," wondering where she might be without them.

Brad spits a little air, "For what?"

Charles adds, "We're true to cause." He slams on brakes for a traffic light.

Gerry can see and feel Charles's vexation, something seldom displayed. She watches him put both hands on wheel and sigh long.

This route is usually a relaxed, unhindered cruise between well-timed traffic signals, but on this day, congestion dominates, and lack of motion and direction persists for car after car. For them, Bessemer's main drag operates as anything but reliable super-highway.

"What the—what is going on?" asks Charles.

Gerry answers low, "It's onlookers coming to gawk—to see a train wreck."

Brad says, "To share excitement, I suppose. Turn here, 'Phe, and go down that road and take a right." They do, and they cut through downtown Bessemer. In a few minutes, they approach Bessemer General's front entrance.

Charles, pleased with progress and Brad's guidance, pulls up in a temporary space out front, an emergency entrance. "You're a genius, H. B, watch me." He jumps out and goes in, leaving motor running. He enters a white brick three story building through marble columns, ornate with molding.

Gerry and Brad remain seated outside, her middle and he right, radio off.

"So how you been, Gerry? I haven't seen you two in a long time."

"Fine, Brad, fine— 'til now."

"Robert been okay?"

"Yes, always Robert. Years have flown since we all met, more than a decade now. You've been busy."

"I have. We all have. I just returned from Pittsburgh. The company considered moving me, but not now. Wife and kids, I guess." He reaches across and kills engine. "Let's go see if we can help 'Phe find out what's happening. This place looks like a beehive."

Charles opens driver door and hops back in before they can move. "I don't think Robert's here. I talked to a person in there, but it seems he's not here. Let's go. They say the roads are all tied up and blocked between here and Woodstock. If people would just stay home, that would help."

Gerry catches a hint of tiredness in Brad's voice, but he rises to occasion and announces a plan, as if diabolic, "I know another U. S. Steel employee 'secret' route, Brother. It'll take us south avoiding congestion of Highway 11 and Highway 5's intersection near Woodstock. We," he adds a little formality, "shall enter Woodstock from east using little known secondary roads."

Charles sums, "I told that woman in the hospital I needed help and information. She pointed to a whole crowd of folks, 'bout 50 people milling around in lobby, and told me, 'They all do.'" His Chevy presses on for unknown results and answers.

Country backroads look dark and more crowded than expected but better and a relief from congested major thruways. Getting closer they hit a roadblock, red lights flashing. Charles rolls down his window and shouts over street noise as if unaware of events, "Officer, how you doing? What's going on? Why all this traffic?" He eyes a line of traffic stretching out in front, blocking their route to Woodstock.

For whatever reason, while waving traffic, a highway patrolman decides to answer, "Holiday for one thing. Always a little bad—mostly, it's people going to the big wreck."

Charles, Brad, and Gerry, look to each other, first one then another—lost for answers.

Gerry concludes, "They're just curious—excitement seekers. I've never heard of such a thing."

An unenthused officer recommends, "Why don't y'all just go home. If you don't have business out here tonight, just go home."

Brad points to a road. "I know these roads. The company has a lot of land out here. That way."

Charles takes a mean left, and they all lean. Traffic conditions improve, still busy for middle of nowhere, rolling hills, hollows, and stream beds, several miles east of Second 47's earlier route. Charles swerves to left lane and passes a slow-moving pickup.

Gerry lies her head back.

They drive on in complete silence, save for growl of Charlie's straight-six Chevy with 235 cubic inches. A stripe free country road, tar black top and silver gravel, passes under headlights. She closes her eyes.

Brad says, "So, you said you do remember when you first met Robert and me, Gerry. I do to some degree."

She didn't open her eyes, "I do, I do well."

November 25 wanes abundant in misnomer and misrepresentation: typical run to Meridian, luxurious streamlined passenger service, wise old engineer, perfect autumn day, peaceful hamlet, superhighway, polite onlookers, helpful hospital attendant, tranquil backroads, pleasant Sunday drive, enjoyable holiday, happy Thanksgiving weekend.

A lot of folks, Gerry and Robert's brothers included, just want to know who's alive and who isn't.

Gerry breaks thought, "Y'all didn't stay long, just walked off. I didn't see Robert again for almost a year. He came traipsing down 55th Street to my house. He had his job and going to Howard College. But Lucille and I talked about y'all all the time. We thought y'all were keepers—good looking, smart—worldly."

"Mercy," Brad's hands have Robert's little quake, "we knew nothing of this world, Gerry. We were fresh out of high school."

They approach a glow of Green Pond proper equating less at night than in day, only a few houses—but some light.

They come to a fork, and Charles angles right across tracks and past yellow railroad crossing warning road signs.

"You're going wrong, 'Phe. This takes you back to Highway 11 and all that craziness. Go this other way," he points down a country road, left and southwest. "Take it, and you're in Woodstock in a whistle."

Charles stops his car, centered on tracks, the Alabama Great Southern Railroad, the Southern—Birmingham to Tuscaloosa. They all look to their left from driver's side, up the grade Cecil, Robert, Pape, and Second 47 took into Woodstock almost ten hours before. Unknowingly, they stare right at trackside Signal 1699—now red. They each focus, even squint. Darkness encroaches on both sides of track, an obscure right of way and moon shadowy rail but at end of their field of vision, where track curves, they can see a few strange light movements of lanterns and headlamps carried and worn by ground emergency and rescue personnel. And they see a glow coming over horizon.

Gerry mutters what they all realize, "We're there."

Charles backs up to proceed as his navigating brother suggests.

She adds, "Poor Daddy," speaking of her father and closes her eyes again, maybe hiding.

Charles slings gravel reversing and turning.

Gerry has known and felt sounds of trains and railroad all her life, long before Robert. As a child and teen, in her bedroom, windows open or closed, she lay awake and listened to steam locomotives, passenger and freight, running a few blocks away. She loved old steam locomotive whistles, and she listened and waited for her daddy to come home from working evenings in railyards, getting off a streetcar and walking three blocks home. Regardless of a day's event—good, bad, or indifferent—when she heard Eugene's foot hit her front porch, she knew it all to be okay. Everything was all right in her world. A young girl went to sleep unaware and uncaring of what some might consider his—or most anyone's—small position in life. For her, his being home solved any problem or worry.

She wishes it still did.

"I must." Charles has to urinate, so he pulls up a slag road by tracks. Gerry and Brad remain seated facing southwest, down rail, toward Woodstock. They continue to watch handheld emergency lights moving in distance. All three realize uncertainty of what awaits short and long term. They realize their insignificance, susceptibility, and helplessness.

Dewfall comes early. Stars above multiply by thousands in clear, low humidity sky—away from city and town—in a rural setting split by a single rail.

Brad remembers, "Gerry, I thought you and I might get together—on that first day when we all met and even later, at the Slipper." He grins—slight, drawing on charm.

"I did too, Brad," still watching activity down tracks, "but it worked out for Robert and me and you and Martha Ann. It all works out. Things work out."

"They do."

Gerry revisits, "Robert does like to talk more though. Now we can't get him to shut up. He found out how much fun talking was."

They parallel tracks, Second 47's earlier route, around a few bends and into Woodstock and a line of cars, more inquisitors with little else to do—idling, inching through town.

Much as before, a Bibb County deputy sheriff waves cars with his flashlight, trying to make everyone move on. He shakes his light in fast flicks, results questionable.

Charles rolls down his window again, "Excuse me, officer, our brother—her husband—was on that train," pointing more to sky.

"Can't stop here. Keep moving. No stopping here," his arm and light still gyrating and directing.

"But where do we go?"

"Pull down by that trooper over there," he points farther down the bumper-to-bumper two-lane. "Go to the crossing and crossroads. He'll tell you what to do. Can't stop here. Keep moving."

They pull forward, stop, and pull forward again as possible, over and over, starting and stopping. To their right, over Brad's shoulder, a couple of gigantic emergency spotlights, erected in haste point up rails northeast of Woodstock.

They ease up to another highway patrolman, a little more receptive than first. Charles repeats about his brother and her husband being on "that train", this time adding, "He was fireman."

His answer comes as before, "You'll have to move on. No stopping here. This all has to be kept clear. Move on."

"Where?"

"On through town. When you hit Highway 5 up there in a mile or so, there's a store, Mayfield's, an information center. But you can't stand still, not here. Emergency vehicles only."

They creep on thru and out of Woodstock. As they rise on a hill west of town center, Charles pulls off on shoulder to relax a minute and regroup and gain perspective. Brad looks back out his window first, followed by Gerry, and Charles. What they see surpasses anything imaginable. They expected it to be strange and ugly but uniqueness and eeriness of such a surreal, haunting scene overwhelms them. Spotlights positioned by station and little general store transmit weird beams in numerous directions illuminating Woodstock's little hollow. For over three-quarters of a mile a ghostlike pale glow spreads northeastward toward Birmingham— over and beyond North Switch—to where tracks curve and Cecil always reduces speed a little. Incandescence offsets ominous shadow, making matters worse. In damning artificial twilight, two trains sit facing each other, engines 50 or 60 feet apart, crumpled and mangled almost beyond recognition.

Unbelievable, my God, unbelievable. They all think same thing.

Rail cars, behind both engines—toy-like and diminutive from above and afar—sprawl both directions in sequence, one going one way, a next pointed another. A car on Second 47, facing southeast, toward Gerry, Charles, and Brad, lodges deep in a mining spur's underpass, running below and across mainline. On 48, facing northeast and away, a coach, third car back, telescoped and appears demolished. Some passenger cars sit on their sides, especially up front, farther back, wheels only derailed. Smoke rises above both engines, spreading forewarning clouds over dozens of ambulance, police, and wrecker lights—swirling red, yellow, and a little blue in haze. Saws whine, drills grind, and winches squeak. A mainline—Birmingham to Meridian, three sidetracks—between Woodstock's North and South Switch, and two mining spurs—to Blocton and West Blocton, all interweave beneath trampling feet of an apparent apparitional, growing throng of humanity. Some come to assist, help, and save, others to observe, gawk, seek souvenirs, or just be a part of something bigger.

Mayfield's Grocery's triage gives hope, maybe some answers. A lot of locals stand in groups throughout parking lot and standing room only conditions prevail inside. Charles squeezes inside to get information, Gerry and Brad stand among interested parties and folks of questionable knowledgeable jawing and killing time in front. Above Mayfield's entrance, an old Barber's Milk clock, a shaggy dog with two tails, one pointing out hours and one minutes, displays—11:30.

A young fellow, maybe 21, with unkempt hair and beard and dirty clothing, barks for a group of eight to ten listeners, so loud Gerry and Brad and most of parking lot overhear. He thunders for his audience, "I'm telling you it was like nothing you never seen before. It was God callin' for reckoning and the devil having his way. When those trains hit, a cloud of something—smoke, or dust or soot or something—went sky high—higher than them trees up there above town and above the church and everything. You should have heard it. I seen a man before it happened—runnin' by the tracks waving something—and another man on a phone right down by that train, and, then they hit. Kaboom! I seen it—from up on the hill there in the grass by the church. I was picnickin', eatin' chips and baloney sandwiches and pickles from right here at Mayfield's."

One shaking head leaves, "His story keeps gettin' bigger and bigger."

Brad asks to no one, "Who is he?"

An onlooker answers, "They call him The Wind. He's always around. He's a nut."

Charles returns, checking out parking lot and speaker. Gerry pulls her sweater tighter around waist, night stiller, darker, chillier, heavy dew on everything including cars. They stand at Mayfield's watching ambulances pass, some have emergency lights and siren on, others head away without flashing light or piercing sound.

Charles informs, "They 'say' Robert was taken to Tuscaloosa. That's all they know or will say. They don't act sure." He goes quiet then, "We'll have to go there."

Brad begs for more, "What's the news, 'Phe? Don't they know? How is he? How is anyone? What's the word? By now you'd think they know something. Seems slow as molasses."

Charles turns his palms upward. "We'll have to go there."

Gerry adds hope, "Good news travels slow."

A white Pure Oil sign with royal blue letters helps light Mayfield's. Gerry from her middle seat examines a Camel cigarette roadside billboard, a cool camel smoking a no-filter stogie. Charles spins wheels again, this time in deep parking lot sand, until rubber meets road. She takes a goodbye look at a fading, blurring peach gibbous moon and shuts big, round eyes once more—they're better closed. She listens to engine groan. Space between highway segments tap a musical click-clack background rhythm, almost as if a train on track. Goodyear rubber spins faster and faster southwest toward Druid City Hospital. She imagines scenarios, who's alive and who isn't, who's injured and who isn't, and who's disabled and who'll be changed forever by a split second of error or dysfunction.

A few miles down road, maybe more, someone's straightforward voice—she's unsure if it's Brad or Charles or Robert—they all like saying it—Mercy.

7

Clarity

National Transportation Safety Board investigations occur for several reasons: to determine what happened, why it did, where responsibility lies, and how to prevent history repeating itself. Unlike court proceedings, NTSB inquiries take place over time. Investigators, attorneys, and various agency and company representatives interview—many times, in some cases—people of interest: participants, witnesses, experts, and concerned parties. Testimonies evolve and change, as memory fluctuation and saving face allows. Facts verify or mitigate; evidence arises and substantiates or refutes. Final goals and outcome exclude conviction, acquittal, and perjury, favoring instead a crystal-clear, when possible, result and picture of event or sequence of events—clarity and, for some, closure in some form or fashion. Most hearings begin by everyone wishing everyone else good luck.

After weeks of statements, questions, answers, interviews—in hospital and out—and innuendo, NTSB's investigation of facts related to head-on collision of Train No. 48 and Train Second No. 47 takes place on December 14 and 15, 1951, in Birmingham's Southern Railway Transportation Building, 1st Avenue North and 22nd Street. A green Southern Railway sign sits atop Southern Railway's ash gray and brick, ten story structure—facing tracks in one direction and Terminal Station in another.

Twenty-some-odd railroad and regulatory officials attend, including vice-presidents, bureaucrats, attorneys, superintendents, technicians, mechanics, union representatives, and one outnumbered court reporter. They hold permanent seats, in two rows around a spacious, but crowded, black walnut conference table. Another 35 or so employees, involved participants, witnesses, and co-workers join a crowded scene—invited to stay in an adjacent auxiliary conference area and hall until called upon. A couple of dozen friends and friends of friends, family, and interested parties gather with them or come and go during a monotonous wait. An occasional news person visits.

All participants keep a somber tone, and most wear business suits, various shades of gray and brown, with white shirts and red and blue ties—Southern's green garb left at home in closet, saved for another day. Their meeting area looks typical: table of about 22 feet length and nine width; front row seats, tan leather, plush, and swiveled; and second tier, army surplus and folding. Seat assignment, as with most things, depends on status. A few people lean against walls, near frequently used escape routes for air, tobacco, and personal comfort.

Walnut paneling covers lower walls up to about three feet, upper walls painted flat white below a cream colored, cracking 12-foot ceiling. A row of four windows comprises one wall, others barren except for a picture on each: a 1946 coal hauling steam locomotive; a new, glistening green and white Southern E8 diesel locomotive, much as those wrecked; and Birmingham's Terminal

Station, a glorious Southern Railway concept and accomplishment. Each picture carried a gold plate description underneath, footnoted by "The Southern Serves the South". One unknown wall-leaning spectator noticed a timely peculiarity and told another, "Ain't no pictures of no wrecks."

Gerry knew Second 47's story all too well, and it makes her sick to think of it again, but maybe cumulative official discourse differs, and she hopes to God, being here, as so many say, offers some relief and helps gets things straight and put to rest once and for all. And she needs to support a process, Robert, their friends and coworkers, and for once herself.

She came in their Dodge pickup, stopping by Hershey to touch base with her despised boss, excused herself, and arrived 15 minutes early. She sits on a second-row metal folding chair provided for family. Her activity level of late surprises her—without alternative, amazing what one does. In front of her on row one, for witnesses, a railroad man checks his Hamilton, she scoots right a little in seat to see—8:58. She succumbs to exhaustion and lost sleep and closes her eyes again, something she seldom does since riding, night of wreck, to Druid City Hospital with Charles and Brad. She reflects on her 20 days equating Halifax, "Poor Mama," thinking of Emma. Gerry kept her office job throughout, took care of two kids with little money, cooked and cleaned, and ran her life without husband input or unwanted guidance. When this is all over—she thinks—I don't know what.

ICC Chief Inspector Smith calls meeting to order, "It's 9 A.M, we should begin. We thank you all for coming." She opens her eyes to a wiry man build and with thick wavy black hair and matching wide mustachio fit for pizza king. His seriousness and etiquette demand attention. He explains meeting's purpose and procedures and opens floor for any opening statements. He and other officials intend to interview, as needed and interchangeably, by popping questions toward interviewees.

Gerry shuts her big peepers again. She'd heard it all, up and down the line, from friends, officials, participants, lawyers, railroad folks, newspapers, TV, even her father and Mr. Street. After leaving Green Pond, Second 47 topped hill and curved into Woodstock. Road Foreman Pape jumped up first—

Mr. Smith interrupts her recall, "The first person to be called today is W. J. Sullivan, conductor on Train No. Second 47."

Court Reporter Hale, one of few women present, rises and goes into hallway to fetch Sul', who by most all accounts, didn't look too darned happy about being first to have to go up there and answer, in front of everybody, a bunch of asinine questions, about who in tarnation knows what, that he mostly answered before. Court Reporter Hale wears a navy dress almost to her ankle, pleated in front with white choir-girl collar. Her brunette, straight hair reaches below her ears. She types, sits, and walks a controlled, professional manner.

Superintendent Shults, thinning salt and pepper hair and protruding nose, begins, "Mr. Sullivan, were you serving as Train Conductor on Second No. 47 on November 25, 1951?" He picks up a thick, round, black fountain pen and begins to make notes and mark reminders off his yellow legal pad.

Sul' feels lost, "Yes, sir."

From that point, questions become general of all interviewees: What time you were called, what time you reported, did you have various trainings and certificates, did you have prescribed rest, how is your health, who did you see and talk to, was anything out of ordinary, and so on for quite some time.

Gerry knows many local conductors as well as anyone, some of their wives her best friends, but she only knows Sullivan's name.

She had heard Robert mention it before in his lengthy company and union phone calls.

"Mr. Sullivan, in addition to yourself, on November 25, your crew consisted of C. S. Love, Engineer, R. M. Gambrell, Fireman, and E. B. Walters, Baggageman, did it not? Were they all in normal condition and in good health, and did you talk to them all?"

"Yes, sir."

"Anyone else?"

"Yes, sir, our flagman, and there was Sam Pape—Road Foreman—S. M. Pape."

Gerry hears his name and thinks of him every day since wreck. She whispers, S. M. Pape.

"What time did Second 47 depart Birmingham Terminal?"

"1:55."

"That was 10 minutes late on the call and 20 minutes behind First 47's regular schedule?"

"Yes, sir." Sul' relaxes some.

"Did you or Engineer Love stop Second 47 after leaving Birmingham's terminal?"

"Well, after we backed through the puzzle switches, just out of the yard."

"And between the puzzle switches at Birmingham and the Burstall switch north of Green Pond, Mr. Sullivan, did you or Engineer Love apply brakes?"

"Yes, sir, Mr. Love applied them at 14th Street—Powderly—north of Bessemer—and let's see, the Woodward Crossing—Bessemer—and at Burstall."

"And the brakes functioned properly and reduce speed?"

"Yes, sir." So, it goes.

"Did you see the signal at Green Pond, north of Woodstock, and was it green?" All these questions are asked of everyone, up and down the line.

"No, sir. I couldn't see it from where I was situated?"

"Do you recall where Second No. 47 was located when the brakes were applied in emergency?"

Sul thinks, scratches his head a little, "Well, I couldn't say for sure. I imagine—well, it was rather a curve there, 10 to 12 passenger car lengths approximately. I wouldn't say as to where it was. I was braced in the seat."

Southern's counsel, Mr. Clark, medium height and lanky, breaks in. Clark wears slicked down chestnut hair. He too has a big dominant nose. His face hangs long, friendly, and deceptive—some said lawyer shifty. "Second 47 was just north of the North Switch at Woodstock when the brakes were applied in emergency, was it not? About 12 car lengths north?"

Sul' answered, "Yes, sir."

Superintendent Shults resumes, "About how fast was Second No. 47 being operated when the brakes were applied in emergency?"

"I would say about 67 to 70 mile per hour."

"What was the maximum authorized speed on that curve?"

Sul considers and decides, "Well, I would have to look at the card. Really, I don't remember."

Counsel Clark interjects, "Will you look at the card and answer that question?"

Sul' refers to a crew timetable and card giving all regulations, times, and speeds for all track sections. "Seventy miles per hour."

Shults takes over again, "Mr. Sullivan, what was the speed of Second 47 when the collision occurred?"

"Forty to forty-five miles per hour."

"You received no serious injury?"

"No, sir."

Shults requests, "Mr. Sullivan, describe what you found after the collision occurred."

Sul breathes a long sigh, thinks, and asks for water. Again, the court reporter, Ms. Hale, obliges while everyone else refers to notes. Mr. Sullivan begins, "Well, me and the flagman off 48, the other train, ran into each other outside my car, and we walked to the rear and into the White Day Coach that the white passengers were in, and I found nobody seriously hurt. There were two or three complaining, one lady particularly, her back was hurting her, and I took it for her husband, or someone with her. I told them to bring her on out through the car there. Then I got on the ground at the rear of the white day coach, and the fireman, my fireman, Bob— Robert Gambrell was lying just about even with the rear of that car. I didn't see, and I left him there and made for the head end." Sul' took another swallow of water.

Most of this sounds almost identical to what everyone's told her. Gerry notices her clinched red hands and wishes she might squeeze out her narrow aisle for a break, but it appears impassable.

"And when I got there, to the head end, to the engine, my engine, there was someone looking in the front end of it and said there was a man trapped in there—but the engine was afire, and no one could get in there to stop it. I spent my time around the head of the diesel engine with fire extinguishers, trying to extinguish the fire and keeping people back away from it, because I was afraid that the oil tank on the engine would blow up and explode."

"Mr. Sullivan, what time did the collision occur?"

"I think it was 2:35."

"You did look at your watch?"

Sul' pulls out his dangling Hamilton, "I did look at my watch, yes, sir." Giving testimony, he dresses casual, free of conductor duds —except his watch, for which he shows endemic pride.

Questions continue about weather, light conditions, what was seen and not seen. All answers indicate everything normal with Sul' up until emergency brake application.

"You were riding fourth car from the engine?"

"Yes, sir."

"And after alighting, you saw Fireman Gambrell on the ground?"

"Yes, sir."

Later in hearing's morning, comes E. B. Walters, baggageman. He receives general questions, as Sullivan had and as all involved parties and witnesses do, before matters become specific.

Shults continues questioning, "Mr. Walters, in earlier interviews, you said before the collision you were in the second engine of Second 47 but decided to go up to the lead engine and then returned back to the second engine. Why?"

"Well, ole Sam Pape came back there so I went up front to see Cecil and Bob."

"Did you have any conversation with the crew members?"

"Sure. We just shot the bull. I don't know why. And, I said I'd go back and get a sandwich, but they said they didn't want no sandwich, so I walked back again. I got back on the rear engine, the second engine, and I was sitting up there eating a sandwich when the brakes went into emergency."

"One reason you were placing yourself in the cab of the second engine was so you could observe your train on curves, was it not?"

"Yes, sir."

"When you left Second 47's lead engine, Mr. Walters, did Engineer Love and Fireman Gambrell appear normal in every respect?"

"Yes, sir."

"Was there anything said with respect to meeting Train No. 48?"

"No, sir."

"So, from the rear engine, on Second 47, when you first saw No. 48 on the main track out front, was it moving or standing still?"

"Standing still."

"When did you realize that the collision would occur?"

Walters rubs his hand through his short, rusty hair. "When he put the brakes on, I looked out, and I saw somebody standing down there. I saw somebody jump off the engineer's side, and it was, 'Katy, bar the door then.'"

Everyone around table repositions and take a moment while questioners regroup and reload.

"Mr. Walters, what effort did you take to protect yourself?"

"I started to jump off. I said, well, if I jump off, I'll get bumped off, so I laid down on the floorboard of the back engine. I laid down on the deck." Gerry hears a few snickers in back and glances toward windows, sunlight, and sky.

"Did you see Mr. Pape leave the engine?"

"Yes, sir, I was looking down when the brakes went on and into emergency."

"Did he descend the steps on the side of the engine or leave it from the—"

Walters answers fast and loud, "I just saw when he jumped off, I don't know. Frankly, I didn't even know who it was. I know somebody jumped off. I didn't know whether it was Pape or Gambrell or who until later on."

"You mean you saw one person leave the engine?"

"Yes, sir."

"Had the brake been applied when you saw this person jump?"

"Done been applied."

"When he jumped?"

"Yes, sir."

"Did you realize that a collision was about to occur?"

"You ain't kiddin'."

"Sir?"

"You are not kiddin'."

Again a few snickers—Walters brings relief, comic or otherwise. In chair or standing, everyone, Gerry included, seems to resituate.

With that—after a long discussion by panel—they break for committee only conference and will meet back after lunch. Most, including railroad executives, walk to the Social Grill for southern meat and three. Each eat for a dollar or less, and discussion centers on specifics of the wreck, weather turning colder since the wreck, and Christmas coming. A few more local types, including Sul' and Walters, venture to Pete's Famous Hot Dogs, iconic dog sauce since early century.

Gerry attends to errands. She goes toward truck but decides on walking to Birmingham Trust National Bank's main office right down street. Banks close at two and since wreck, her family needs resources already. She has just enough time to step into a pharmacy for child supplies.

A few minutes after 1:00, Interstate Commerce Commission Inspector Dansforth calls meeting to order. "Thank you, gentlemen —and few ladies who join us—for your attendance and cooperation. We'll continue by asking Miss Hale, our court reporter, to bring in N. A. Hoadley, conductor on Train No. 48."

Hoadley enters in hurried fashion, imposed upon, a round bodied and red-faced man, probably 50 or so.

Dansforth starts by verifying Hoadley as conductor on northbound 48 out of Meridian heading to Birmingham. He asks same questions asked of Sullivan and Walters about a normal day and operation. As with others, Hoadley found November 25's trip to Woodstock ordinary.

Again, Gerry knew little, if anything, of Hoadley. Robert had his circle of close friends, Hoadley excluded.

Counsel Clark asks, "How many passengers did you have leaving Tuscaloosa?"

"We loaded 55 at Tuscaloosa," his voice booms.

"You had a total of 214 passengers leaving Tuscaloosa?"

"That's right."

"Do you recall, Mr. Hoadley, how many times the speed of your train, No. 48, was reduced by application of brakes between Meridian and the point of the accident?"

"Well, we slowed down through Cuba that I remember, and going into York, and of course, over both bridges, the Tombigbee and Black Warrior, and over a slow order, 8 miles per hour at milepost 191, and then at the signal at the South Switch at Woodstock. When we headed in, we slowed down to head in at Woodstock."

"Could you tell that the speed of your train at these locations was reduced by the engineering applying the brake?"

"Could I what?" He looks irritated and leans forward.

"Tell that the speed of the train was reduced by an application of the brake valve?" Clark stands and comes closer.

"Yes, sir."

"By the engineer?"

Hoadley nods, "Yes, sir, you can always tell."

"So far as you know then the brakes were functioning properly?"

"That's right."

"Do you recall, Mr. Hoadley, what time Train No, 48, your train, passed the South Switch at Woodstock?"

Hoadley sits back and crosses his hands on his chest. "Well, somewhere around 2:30. I don't remember just exactly because we slowed down and headed in and I heard him blow signals and I got up and went and looked at First 47. First 47 had stopped on the main line waiting for us, 48, to take the sidetrack. I stood there and rode as we went down the passing track down to the little

Woodstock station. After that, I looked up the track and didn't see anything, and went and sat back down. I had a lot of work to do, and when we stopped, I took it for granted we was standing in the clear. I never had any idea at all otherwise."

"Do you remember at what speed your train, 48, was traveling when it entered the South Switch at Woodstock?"

"Oh, I imagine 10 or 15 miles an hour. I couldn't tell just exactly."

"Did you state that the engineer on First 47 blew signals?"

Hoadley leans forward again, "He did." Signals warn of a second train following behind. Signals usually consist of one long and two shorts.

"At 48, your train? He blew signals at 48?"

"He did. Yes, sir."

"Did anyone on Train 48, your train, answer the signal?" Rules require a whistle response to signals, sometimes two shorts.

"No, sir, I never heard it."

"Mr. Hoadley, about what speed did your train, No. 48, maintain between the station at Woodstock until about the time it stopped?"

"Oh, I imagine 10 or 15 miles per hour, I couldn't just exactly say how fast. My mind wasn't even on the speed." Hoadley takes out a white, folded handkerchief and wipes his forehead.

Gerry thinks, he seems inconvenienced.

"If the speed had been excessive though you would have noticed that?"

"Oh, yes, sir, I would have."

"Mr. Hoadley, what is your understanding of the speed that can be made by a train when on the siding at Woodstock or any other siding?"

"They are supposed to go through at a restricted speed, you know."

"Do you mean, Mr. Hoadley, that the restricted speed is at reduced speed or at yard speed?"

"That's right."

Mr. Clark, standing, puts his hand on hips and walks toward Hoadley, "Which one of them now?"

"Well, yard speed is in the passing tracks, you know."

"You are familiar with Rule 105 of the Book of Operating Rules that governs the speed through sidings, are you not?"

"Yes, sir."

Mr. Shults, Superintendent of the Alabama Great Southern Railroad, rises again and interrupts, "At this time I would like to read Rule No. 105 into the investigation: 'Unless otherwise provided, trains or engines using sidings or yard track must proceed at yard speed.'"

Mr. Clark asks, "What is yard speed, Mr. Hoadley, I mean your understanding of it?"

"Well, I couldn't—I don't remember exactly, but about 10 miles per hour, I imagine, or so you can stop in the range of your vision or a car length." Hoadley looks lost.

Mr. Shults interjects again, "At this time, I will read into the investigation a definition of yard speed: 'Yard speed is the speed that will permit stopping within one-half the range of vision.'"

Mr. Clark resumes, "Mr. Hoadley, when Train 48, your train, came to a stop, you were what?"

"Still working."

"Occupying space provided for the conductor's office?"

"That's right," still clutching handkerchief.

"How long did you remain in this location, Mr. Hoadley, after the train stopped?"

"Well, I couldn't tell just exactly how long it was. I hadn't gotten down good until the crash came. I fell out in the aisle, and after I went out in the aisle, I got up and pushed the tickets all up in a corner so they wouldn't be destroyed."

Clark cuts him off, "Mr. Hoadley, you received no injury in connection with the accident?"

Hoadley wipes his nose, "Well, I am still sore in the back and hips, and my neck is all stiff."

"Outside of the soreness though and the bruise or two, you received no serious injury."

Hoadley moves in his chair and takes a drink of water, "No sir. No, sir."

"You were able to look after the passengers as well as you could?"

"I stayed right there with them for hours and the most unusual part of it was, I collapsed down here on 20th Street in front of the Southern Railway office."

Clark goes back to his seat, pauses, picks up his pad, continues standing, and asks, "Mr. Hoadley, the two cars most damaged on your train were the two head cars?"

"That's right."

"The damage to these cars was caused by Coach 833, the Colored Car, telescoping Car 700, the combined car?"

"That's right."

"Can you give us an estimate, Mr. Hoadley, as to how far Train 48 was moved backwards due to the impact when Train Second 47 collided with it?"

"I imagine 50 or 60 feet. I can't tell just exactly how far, but I know it was something like that."

Following Hoadley, NTSB's panel interviews A. J. McLaurine, flagman on northbound 48. His testimony proceeds pretty much as his conductor's, Hoadley's. At one point, things change and become tense and unusual.

McLaurine may be oldest and most experienced person in room, ancient for a flagman, his face twisted by time, weather, and miles. He dresses old-fashioned railroad—pin stripe overalls, long-sleeved, collared white shirt, work boots, even a matching cap.

Mr. Clark questions, "Mr. McLaurine, in your interviews, you've said over and over that in your opinion, you have an idea that the sun shining on this signal on North Switch at Woodstock caused your engineer, Mr. Pyler, to mistake it or something of that sort. Just for what reason do you think he was mistaken?"

McLaurine answers, "I believe the sun maybe had an effect on him."

"What effect?"

"It would make it look a different color."

"How would it do that?"

"We see it every day on the street, the sun shining through them. Some of them is hard to judge."

Mr. Clark leans back in his chair to think and starts an almost unnoticeable rock, "Yes, but we are talking about railroad signals now, a little different than the traffic signal. If you have any reason for believing that, we would like to know what it is."

McLaurine smiles, cocks his head, and chuckles, "I don't believe the man—Engineer Pyler—went out there, went out and deliberately didn't look at the signal. I believe if anything, he just misjudged the signal. Of course, that is just my mind. Of course, I could be wrong, but I have been working behind him a long time."

Everything in room became motionless and quiet, Gerry stared through this old flagman without emotion or feeling. She scans room, and most everyone does same.

NTSB's hearing adjourns early on its first day. Chief Inspector Smith thanks everyone again for attendance and input and tells everyone he and some others will be refreshing and dining at Dale's Cellar, a basement steakhouse using an original soy and ginger marinade. Visitors love it. "Oh, Mr. Kirchner of the L&N Railroad just told me he will host some of his people at Joy Young's," founded by non-English speaking Chinese in boomtown Birmingham early century.

Smith closes by saying he and other officials had things to work on and, "Tomorrow, we start 8 AM sharp. We need to speak with Fireman Alass and at a least a couple of witnesses with bystander accounts, and we have two people joining us from local hospitals—one right after lunch and one about 3 PM or later. Expect a long day." Smith finishes with one of Day One's few, if any, smiles.

Their pickup takes Gerry back to her parents' home. Since wreck, Emma helps her get older son in and out of school, keeps younger while Gerry works, and they all stay warm and well fed. For Gerry, staying in Woodlawn, instead of at her and Robert's home on Willow Lane, reduces many miles of commute to and from inner city. Eugene enjoys kids though he fails to admit it. Life goes on.

Willow Lane must wait. Things changed without Robert coming and going. She had been there once since wreck.

As promised, Day Two begins without ceremony or delay. Chief Inspector Smith again turns questioning over to Mr. Clark, his thin and bright face welcome to all—except interviewees. Clark impresses as personable, and honest—for a lawyer. Maybe, 'cause he didn't participate in private practice, some theorize. But when he asks questions, he transforms to beast.

Congregation increases as more come from near and far to support, spectate, and gossip. In what some call odd circumstance, a whole crowd of folks, central Alabama railroaders and friends, descends on Southern Railway's building. They line hallways, stand on steps out front—shaking hands, discussing, visiting, and well-wishing—good-intentioned community spirit, exacerbated by still so little TV.

At 8:01, Chief Inspector Smith begins, "L.M., all yours."

Clark rises, wearing a tailored, brown worsted suit and golden striped necktie, straight from a D.C. haberdasher.

Miss Hale, Court Reporter, dressed business as before, steps out and calls Fireman C. R. Alass.

Clark begins with standard questions again followed by, "Mr. Alass, you were serving as Fireman on Train No. 48 out of Meridian, heading to Birmingham, on November 25, were you not?"

"Yes, sir." Alass, as others, had done preliminary questions and sessions. He knows what to expect and looks sheepish from git-go. As Conductor Hoadley before him, he seeks water.

"How long have you been following this assignment?"

"That particular day with Mr. Pyler was my first trip, but I had been on 47 and 48 for about three and a half months."

"The record shows, Mr. Alass, that you were born on November 7, 1916, and entered service with the Alabama Great Southern Railroad on November 11, 1937?"

"Yes, sir." Alass looks bumfuzzled or shell-shocked, and dresses in work clothes more disheveled than others, wearing a long-sleeved cotton shirt, wrinkled and checked brown and yellow and crumpled tan pants. His light brown hair spreads onto his forehead. His features strike observers as ordinary, but his skin looks pock-marked and ragged for his age—but uneasy describes him best. It has been a long three weeks.

Clark continues his list of general questions asked of all, including, "Do you know that the brakes were properly tested at Meridian?"

"Yes, sir."

"You had an opportunity to observe and talk with your engineer, Mr. Pyler, both before and after leaving Meridian, and did you notice anything unusual about him?"

"No, sir, nothing unusual."

"He was normal in every respect?"

"Normal in every way."

"Had you fired for Engineer Pyler before?"

"No, sir."

Clark rolls on, "After your train, No. 48, passed Vance, which is first station south of Woodstock, where was the first signal you encountered that was displaying other than a proceed indication?"

"I don't recall the number of that signal—the distance of that signal down there—below the South Switch of Woodstock."

"It was the first northbound signal then south of the South Switch at Woodstock?"

"At Woodstock, yes, sir."

"That signal was displaying an approach indication?" Clark still stands erect, in one place.

"Yes, sir." Alass rubs his hands on his creaseless, tan trousers.

"Did you call the indication to the attention of Mr. Pyler?"

"Yes, sir."

"Did Mr. Pyler acknowledge the signal?"

"He did."

"Did Mr. Pyler reduce the speed of his train according to the indication of the signal?"

"Yes, sir."

"How was the weather, approaching Woodstock?"

"Clear."

"Was the visibility good?"

"Yes, sir."

"Sun shining bright, as has been stated?"

"Yes, sir."

"When you pulled into the siding at south end of Woodstock, did you see First 47 on the main track?"

Taking a drink of water and setting down his cup, "At the south end, I did. Yes, sir, he was on the main line waiting for us to pull into the siding."

"Did First 47 blow signals—indicating to you that a second train followed behind his train?"

"Yes, sir."

"Did he have green signals (green flags on each front engine flank) displayed—indicating to you that a second train followed?"

"Yes, sir."

"Did Mr. Pyler acknowledge the signals blown by First 47?"

"Yes, sir."

"Mr. Alass, had you heard any discussion about the Crescent being detoured as Second 47 and following First 47?"

"Yes, sir."

"Did you and Pyler discuss this detour?"

"No, sir."

"You don't know whether Mr. Pyler knew it—that Second 47 had been detoured?"

"He knew there was going to be a Second 47."

"Did Mr. Pyler comment on Second 47 after First 47 blew signals for you?"

"Yes, sir."

"What did he say with respect to Second 47?"

"'I wonder if we are going to get away for Second 47.'"

"Was that all Engineer Pyler had to say in moving up through the siding?"

"Yes, sir."

"Did you continue to sit in the fireman's seat?"

"Yes, sir."

"When did you get up from the fireman's seat?"

"When we passed the dwarf signal, at the North Switch where we were to get back out on the main line." A dwarf signal measures about four feet in height as opposed to tall signals, above an engine crew's eye level, at about 15 feet. This dwarf signal served as only and last barrier to 48 exiting its siding and taking the main line north toward Birmingham.

"Did you call the indication of the dwarf signal to Mr. Pyler?"

"Yes, sir."

"As required by the rules?"

"Yes, sir."

"What did you call?"

"A clear signal."

"You mean the light was a green?"

"Green light, yes, sir."

"That meant to proceed?"

"Proceed."

Clark inspects his legal pad while asking, "When did you first see the dwarf signal? At what location was 48's train in the siding when you first saw it and called his indication to Engineer Pyler?"

"We were approaching the dwarf signal. Mr. Pyler says, 'I believe that signal is clear.' I says, 'Yes, I believe it is clear, a green light.'"

"Where were you located exactly when you said this?"

"Shy of the dwarf signal there."

"How far away?"

"Several car lengths there." Alass begins to squirm and bob in clarity's hot seat, placing hands on knees.

Clark moves and creeps around, some later likened him to an industry employed Perry Mason. "You made no effort to look at the dwarf signal until you were three or four car lengths south of the dwarf signal?"

"I could see the signal from quite a distance there."

Clark paces to a window and looks out on First Avenue and raises volume more than needed, "Forty-eight's engine was somewhere between Woodstock's station and the North Switch when you first observed the dwarf signal?"

"Yes, sir."

Clark continues looking outside, "When did Mr. Pyler first say to you that he believed the signal was clear?"

"We were somewhere below the switch there—before we got back out on the main line."

"At that time, Mr. Pyler was maintaining a speed of what?" Clark returns moving toward Alass, in his seat.

"About 15 MPH."

"Could you see the speedometer?"

"No, sir, I just estimated it."

"Mr. Pyler's first statement about the dwarf signal was made south of the North Switch where you went back on the main line?"

"Yes, sir."

Clark stands above Alass, "What were his exact words?"

"Just exactly what I said, 'I believe that that signal is clear.'"

"What did you reply to it?"

"I told him I believe that signal is clear too, a green light."

"Was the signal clear or green?"

"The signal was clear."

Clark walks away again, "Or did you just believe it was clear?"

"The signal was clear."

"It continued to be green until when?"

"The last time I saw it, it was still clear."

"You were right on the signal?"

"Yes, sir."

"The last time you saw it, it was clear?"

"It was green."

Clark stands behinds his own chair, hands on headrest, "Are you positive it was clear?"

"I am positive that it was a green light."

Mr. Clark sits down, and Superintendent Shults takes over again. Shults shares Clark's dignified manner but lacks flare and charisma. He appears honest, frank, and helpful.

"When did you, Mr. Alass, first realize the North Switch was aligned for the main line, for Second 47 going north and south—not for 48, your train, on the sidetrack?"

"I just raised up in my seat and was standing up, just took a notion for some unknown reason to stand up, and was propped up against the windshield, just looking out the windshield there, and I discovered that the switch was lined for the main line."

"That was after 48, your engine, passed the dwarf signal?"

"Yes, sir."

"Did Engineer Pyler, going through the siding, maintain a lookout ahead?"

"Yes, sir."

"You and Mr. Pyler were not doing anything on the engine that would distract your attention from the job at hand?"

"No sir."

"The only conversation you had after you passed Woodstock Station was in connection with the signal?"

"Yes, sir."

"There was nothing on the train that distracted your attention?"

"No, sir."

"Did Mr. Pyler still seem normal in every respect?"

"Yes, sir."

"Mr. Alass, what did you do or say when you saw the switch was set for the main track instead of the siding?"

"I told him to put the brake immediately, put the automatic brake valve in first service application."

"So far as you could tell, did he get the desired results from the brake?"

"Yes, sir."

"Where were you exactly when you saw the switch was aligned against you, 48, and for Second 47?"

"I believe we were just—we were just about the frog. Yes, sir, we were maybe a little south of the frog there, Mr. Shults, standing up in the cab, and looking at the switch points, looking out that way—" A frog is exact point in a switch where one rail disappears and another begins, where a train wheel jumps from one track to another.

"You, as fireman, called a warning to Engineer Pyler?"

"Yes, sir."

As on cue, Shults sits, appearing tired, and Clark returns rejuvenated. Alass rubs his forehead and pushes back hair, scanning wall to wall, seat to seat, among a crowd grown standing room only —another person's chances of being squeezed inside nonexistent. Someone in back began cracking windows for fresh air.

Gerry feels a little sorry for him. A stranger to her, he appears beaten.

Clark attacks giving little time for an Alass regroup, "Mr. Alass, why did you get out and flag after your train had stopped?"

"After finding the switch lined for the main line, I felt that something was wrong, and that I would go up the track to protect the train in case anything else was coming south."

Clark gets up and begins pacing again, in between and around table, as much as a packed room permits. He returns and stands by his empty chair, puts on reading glasses, looks at his notes, and places his pad on table—glasses on top. "It never occurred to you Second 47 was coming to Woodstock from the north to meet your train, 48?"

"No, sir."

"The fact First 47 blew signals at you didn't mean Second 47 was coming?"

"That's right."

Gerry detects a few spectator coughs.

"Mr. Alass, if you are positive your signal was green, why did you immediately get out to protect 48, your train?"

"Just for safety's sake, after finding the switch wrong, I felt like something had gone wrong somewhere or other." Alass releases a long sigh.

"What did you use for flagging?"

"I had a big orange rag or red flag, what we call a 'orange rag', one of those big wiping rags on the diesel."

"How long after your train, 48, stopped did you start to flag?"

"Immediately."

"Did you run or just walk?"

"I started off walking in a good hurry."

"How far had you walked 'in a hurry' until you saw Second 47 coming?"

"Well, I don't recall exactly how far. I had walked quite a little distance there, and I was looking up the track and saw Second 47 when she came into where you could see it from walking up the track, when it came around the curve, and I immediately broke and ran up the track facing southbound Second 47, as hard as I could run. And when the cab of the engine had got where it could see me, where I figured it could see me, I was waving this rag across the track as hard as I could wave it."

"Did the engineer on Second 47 acknowledge your signal?"

"Yes, sir." Cecil gave her two short whistle blasts.

"Mr. Alass, when did you last see your engineer Mr. Pyler?"

"The last time I saw Mr. Pyler was when he got out of the cab of the engine."

"Did you get out of 48's engine first or did Pyler?"

"I believe I got down on the ground first, yes, sir, because I was standing on my seat."

"There is no doubt in your mind that the dwarf signal was clear?"

"That's right."

"Still, you told Mr. Pyler you thought it was clear?"

"Clear, green light."

Clark sits and reads again, "At this time, Mr. Alass, I would like to ask you about a statement you made on November 27 to Mr. M. E. Strunk, General Road Foreman of Engines. At that time, it does not appear you were definite that the signal was clear, you just thought it was clear, isn't that true?"

"At that time, I was just asked to make a statement of what happened. I asked if it was an investigation, and he told me that there wasn't anyone there to make an investigation."

"Why did you not state in the statement that you were positive the signal was clear, instead of you thought it was clear?"

"Because I knew there would be a time when the investigation would be held properly."

"In other words, you intended at the time you made the statement to say differently from what you were to state on the investigation?"

"Sir?"

"It was your intention all along to withhold facts, in the statement you made on the 27th?"

"Until the proper time."

"Why would you not say definitely—the signal was clear when you made the statement, if it was true?"

"Well, I just figured it was not the proper time, that the proper time would be when the investigation was held."

Gerry loses her sympathy.

Clark stands again, pushing back his seat with his legs, "I ask you once more, you are positive the dwarf signal was clear?"

"Yes, sir."

Clark pulls his chair back under and sits down. ICC Inspector P. C. Smith stands to ask a question. He dresses in shirt and tie, a young man who speaks dry, squeaky, high tones. He lives by facts. "Mr. Alass, after the collision occurred did you get on the telephone and call the train dispatcher?"

"Yes, sir."

"I wish you would relate what conversation you had with the train dispatcher."

"I told him to send all the ambulances possible, that No. 48 and Second 47 had had a head-on collision, and there was a lot of people hurt, and that there was some cars telescoped, some down on the L & N mine track below, and two diesel engines tore all to pieces."

"Did you or did you not tell the dispatcher that your engineer mistook or 'We mistook the signal,' this dwarf signal, was the reason your train was on the mainline?"

"I don't remember discussing any signal at all with the dispatcher."

Inspector Smith sits down, "All right."

Superintendent Shults asks, while sitting, "Mr. Alass, did you have flagman's signals on the engine, red flag, fusees?"

"Yes, sir, I had a red flag and fusees on there."

"Were they accessible?"

"Yes, sir."

"Why did you not use them? You said you used an orange rag to flag? Why?"

"Well, I just had it in my hand when I got off."

Mr. Clark joins again, "Is it possible that you could have told the dispatcher when you reported the accident to him that you and Engineer Pyler mistook the indication displayed by the signal, and just don't recall it—at this time?"

Alass looks through glazed eyes, "I don't say that it is impossible, no, sir. I just don't believe that I discussed any indication of the signal with the dispatcher."

"It is possible that you could have done so?"

"It is possible."

"And you just don't recall it at this time?"

"It is possible."

Chief Inspector Smith elevates, looks at his wristwatch—11:50. "We'll recess for lunch. This afternoon, we'll have others, as I said before. Mr. Alass, please stay, we may need you again. I went to Social Grill yesterday and Dale's last night, I'm ready for a hot dog today." Smith and Superintendent Shults exchange pleasantries and smiles—something absent in Southern offices for quite some time. Shults, as most, still finds it challenging.

8

I Come to Testify

By mid-December, Alabama weather conditions risk deterioration. Everyone hurries out for lunch wearing popular and trendy long trench coats—tan, black, green, blue, and gray, wool or rayon blend, cut below knees, with wide pointed collars and two rows of large, shiny buttons. Winds whip up and down Birmingham's older sections causing noon day pedestrians to lean forward to overcome headwinds. Fashion includes headwear, people holding on tight.

Navigating city and parking a straight stick 1950 pickup becomes cumbersome in a hurry. Gerry rolls through Southside to check in at work for messages and appease her always grouchy boss. She hates few in life, but he rates as one. She has time to dart into a sandwich shop. Other than an updraft up skirt, things go fine. Eating while driving takes concentration and constant wariness. A dropped glob of pimento cheese might mar her pretty, green print dress Emma gave her.

Gerry arrives when meeting reconvenes at 1:00 for second day's afternoon session. She uses a side door off 22nd Street and steps into a foyer and a who's who of Southern Railway employees and union representatives. Looking around she asks herself, "What is everyone doing here? Still just curious, I guess." Some in attendance come because they must, others have peculiar, hard to figure need. She sees Red Duncan and Wilder Barnes, two of Robert's best friends, who as local union reps as well as employees, sat through yesterday's meeting and have reason to sit it out to bitter end. Others, good hardworking and concerned railroad people, just want to be there and show backing. She finds strangers and those who look familiar, but names evade. Some knowledgeable railroad experts and buffs attend, interested in anything and everything rail.

Before Gerry catches breath, Mr. Shults begins herding everyone into an already packed meeting chamber with meeting already in order. They must have begun early.

Mr. Dansforth, a rotund, clammy ICC inspector, asks of P. J. Gray, a Belcher Lumber Company Manager, "Tell us what you did after 48 and Second 47 collided."

Mr. Gray has stated he visited on his mother's porch several hundred feet south. He appears an earnest country gentleman and answers, "They hit behind some trees, and after they crashed, the southbound, Second 47, knocked 48's engine back from behind the trees so I could see. I went to call for help from the store, then went back to the wreck."

"How did you go to call?"

"In my car. I drove up to the store and back."

"And what did you do then?"

"Someone said there's someone trapped in the engine—of the southbound. And, I went, and we tried to get him out but couldn't. We could talk to him but couldn't get him out."

After a few last general questions and pleasantries of Gray, Ms. Hale, still proper and controlled—makeup and hairspray fading —calls in L. F. Wade, a cement finisher who lived in Woodstock and happened to be strolling by the track and sidings with his wife and friend. Shults ask more trivial questions before his main one for Wade, "And when you looked at the northbound signals, those displayed for 48, what were they displaying?"

Wade answers, "All red."

A few minutes and one interviewee later, Shults asks I. G. Cash, dispatcher at the Terminal Station in Birmingham at time of accident, "You did get indications on your board when First 47 passed the North Switch at Woodstock and when 48 passed the South Switch? And you noted the times on your train sheets?"

Cash, a dainty, balding, black horned rimmed, middle-aged technician, "Yes, sir."

"What were those times?"

"First 47 hit the North Switch at 2:25. Forty-eight hit the South Switch at 2:31."

"How do you know when the accident occurred?"

"I looked at my board and there was a white light on in the North Switch lever that indicated it was out of line, and I mentioned to the Chief Dispatcher that something was wrong."

"What time was that?"

"2:35."

Clark, fresh as a daisy and sharp, even after dinner, rises and asks, "At 2:35 PM, you had an indication on the switch lever that the switch was not set properly. Is that right?"

"Yes, sir, that something was wrong."

"What was your first indication of the accident?"

"Fireman Alass called me and told me about it."

Clark moves toward windows again, moving behind the row of officials sitting at the table. He stops and looks out, "What did Mr. Alass say?"

"He said the signal looked clear to them. The first words was they mistook the signal, that it looked clear to him and Engineer Pyler both, and he saw they were wrong before they got on the switch, and he hollered for Mr. Pyler to Big Hole (apply emergency brake), but he said he was too late to stay out of the switch, and he jumped off to try to flag the other man, and he was too late to do that." Cash relaxes, and everyone remains quiet, including Clark who meanders back to his chair, puts hands on its back, looks around at almost every face one at a time, then walks to a chalk board and writes in large, plain numerals and letters:

Time 48 in siding   4 minutes
Yard speed limit required of #48   15/mph
Time required to travel 1 mile @ 15mph/   4 minutes
Length of siding at Woodstock
between South and North Switches 1.62 miles

Clark avoids speaking, he simply steps back and reviews his work, goes to his seat, rubs his hands along sides of his head, and waits for Shults to announce a break. Everyone sits still, some examining his figures, others working them out for themselves on scratch paper. A few walk up to study closer, and some ask others what it means.

As people exit for their well-deserved breather, Shults reminds them, "There's still much to get to and do today. We'll only break for a few, and we'll finish up by 5, maybe, if we're lucky."

Gerry steps out to ladies' room and back into hall for water from a ceramic fountain's silver spout, turning a matching shiny, chrome knob with four nodules. Gerry sips, finding it refreshing, Thanks, I needed that—or as Robert might say, Cool, clear agua. She turns around, centered in hall outside conference room, and recognizes dozens of faces from all over the railroad. Most ignore her, look right past her, and watch something else—a man entering off First Avenue.

Man of hour arrives, striding as if urgent and great things await. His wife accompanies by his side. He walks straight up and tall, speaking and nodding to well-wishers along his path, as if a presidential candidate or international dignitary. He advances straight toward Gerry. If he feels embarrassed by attention, he shows little, if any, sign. He excuses himself beyond a person or two in front, steps to Gerry, and gives her a warm hug, as best he can with a bandaged hand as big as a microwave oven. He smiles ear-to-ear and throws both arms around her in a bear hug, "Geraldine."

Hugging his neck, she rests both hands on his shoulders, "Look at you." She holds him arm length, "Just look at you. It is so good to see you, Cecil. So good."

He almost flinches at her grasp, his aging body, far from its best. "Geraldine, so good to be here," and marches on. He looks weak, wobbly, but healthy, all things considered. True victories in life number few.

C. W. Cottrell and Frank Sparks, dearest friends and some of last to see Robert before Second 47 went out to Meridian, greet Engineer Love and shake his good hand, his left.

Cecil's voice, shaky but booming with excitement, declares to all, "I'm just happy to be here," drawing laughter and a sense of relaxation from folks milling around, and as he enters meeting room, "I come to testify."

Mr. Shults returns, "Mr. Love, you may take your seat."

Once everyone sits, Mr. Clark reemerges, "Mr. Love, the record indicates you were born on July 24, 1897, and that you entered the service with the Alabama Great Southern Railroad on March 5, 1913, and you were promoted to engineer on June 7, 1937. Is that correct?"

"Yes, sir."

Clark remains seated and gives Cecil his name, rank, and serial number questions—preliminary information needed—so repetitive and mundane now, everyone knows them and answers before Clark asks them, as if opening a ceremony with pledge of allegiance. Clark covers ground faster than Cecil goes downhill and he saves best for last until he slows and asks, "Mr. Love, the first automatic signal for southbound trains north of Woodstock is at Green Pond. Do you picture that signal and know its location?"

"Yes, sir, I know right where it is."

"Approaching the signal and passing it, it was clear?"

"Clear, yes, sir."

"Passing that signal at Green Pond, Mr. Love, where was Mr. Pape and Mr. Gambrell?"

"Mr. Gambrell was sitting on his seat on the left side of the engine, and Mr. Pape was sitting on the middle seat, but he got down."

"Mr. Love, do you recall what speed you were operating Second 47 rounding the curve north of Woodstock?"

"I couldn't say exactly, but it was approximately 65 miles an hour. I don't know exactly, but it was right in that vicinity."

"The maximum speed authorized on this curve is 70 mile per hour?"

"Yes, sir."

"What was you first knowledge that you had that No. 48 was occupying the main track at the North Switch at Woodstock?"

"As we rounded the curve coming into Woodstock, Mr. Pape jumped up. I'm sure he was under the same impression I was that he was on the passing track, but as we traveled around in due length of time to determine where he was, he hollered, 'My God, he's on the mainline.' That is when I immediately went into emergency, and I could see 48's fireman out in front of the engine signing me down."

"Was Road Foreman Pape the first person on the engine to state or know that No. 48 was on the mainline?"

"He was first to say it, but we realized it about the same time."

Clark leans way back, his seat squealing, and asks, "You immediately applied the brakes in emergency?"

"Yes, sir."

"About how far north of No. 48's engine were you when you realized that 48 was on the mainline?"

"That's purely a guess. I really don't know. I would say probably 40 car lengths or something like that."

"Forty freight cars?" Mr. Clark taps his pen on his pad with every question.

"Yes, sir. Sure not passenger cars. That is purely a guess." Freight cars might measure near 40 linear feet, passenger cars perhaps 60 to 70.

"You saw someone ahead of No. 48's engine that might have been attempting to flag or warn you of the situation."

"Yes, sir. I heard it later, I couldn't determine at that time, didn't know at that time, but I saw 48's fireman out there waving me down in front of the engine. Heard later it was the fireman."

"Was this person who you think to be 48's fireman, was he moving towards you rapidly?"

"No, sir. He was standing in the middle of the track waving."

"About how far ahead of 48's engine was this person who you think was the fireman?"

"This is purely a guess. I would say a car length. Not too far. I couldn't say just how far, but not too far."

"You did take it to be a length of a freight car?"

"Passenger car, I would say."

Clark thinks, "Somewhere, then, between 40 and 80 feet?"

"That's right."

"Was this person who was attempting to sign you down using flag signal?"

"Not that I saw. If he had other flagging equipment, I didn't see it. Of course, he could have had."

"If he had been using a fusee for a stop signal, you would have seen it?"

"Yes, sir, I certainly would have seen it."

"Do you recall when Mr. Pape left the engine?"

"Not exactly, but he was not but just—immediately he left the engine."

"From the fireman's side, the left side?"

"From the right side, the engineer's side. Almost immediately, but I couldn't tell. I was busy there, but almost immediately."

Clark moves his papers and pauses, looking over meeting participants. Cecil sits back and takes a deep breath and blows a long CO2 for all room to hear—as if approaching crossing.

Clark smiles a pleasant acknowledgement and continues, "That was immediately after he saw No. 48 was on the mainline."

"Yes, sir, and I had went into emergency."

"Did Fireman Gambrell leave from the same side?"

"Yes, sir, he left from the right side."

"What, in your opinion, was the speed of your engine, Second 47, when the collision occurred?"

"I would say about 40 miles per hour. I wouldn't know. That is purely a guess."

"Did you make any attempt to leave the engine, Mr. Love?"

Cecil rubs his nose with his left hand and relies on it to unfold his red bandana handkerchief and wipe his forehead. "No, I did not. I tried to go down in the engine room but couldn't get the door open. That's the reason I stayed up in the cab."

Mr. Clark pauses too, drinks some water and gets up to walk around. "Tell us, Mr. Love, in what position were you when the actual impact occurred."

"I was stooping behind the fireman's seat on the left side of the engine. Had hold of the bottom of the seat with one hand and top with the other, stooping down behind it."

"Did you remain conscious after the accident occurred?"

"I did. All the way."

"Could you tell us, in your own words, what happened after the collision occurred?"

"Yes, I can tell you just what took place there. When the impact came, the floor buckled up, which raised me right in the top of the cab. And only thing that I know what happened was that I had a hold of the bottom of the seat with one hand and top with the other and some of the perforated steel in the top of the cab tore loose and came down under the seat. And that is what cut this hand off." He lifts his huge bandage on end of his right arm. "And I believe that is what kept the impact off of me. When it finally settled down, I was kind of dazed, and I went to feel for my glasses, and at that time I discovered my hand was cut off." Again, Cecil breaks, this time just to move in his seat, and go on. His eyes show building moisture, "My feet were fastened and my hips and also my shoulder, and the cut off hand was the only thing free about me, and at that point, I began to holler. The blood was coming out of my hand. There were some passengers then moving around, and I tried to instruct them how to cut the motor down by pushing down on that isolation shaft and holding off the stop button. They told me they had done that, and I told them to go back and push both start and stop buttons, which would more than likely blow a fuse, the main fuse, and stop the motor. At that time, they were getting me out, and somebody, I don't know who, pulled me out the bottom of the windshield. Some sailor came up there and corded my arm. Don't know who he was. That's about as far as I know. They took me out to Bessemer Hospital."

Clark walks to Cecil, "Was your hand completely severed in the accident or was it amputated at the hospital?"

Cecil pulls up his huge, bandaged knub and stares at it, "Completely severed at the time of the accident."

Clark returns to his chair, tosses down his pad and looks to Shults who waves his hand calling recess in a brusque manner, "We'll have another interviewee, and we should be done. For now, everyone has a smoke break."

In corridor, some people disperse, but many linger. Gerry loiters to twin, glass doors and admires First Avenue—more and more people in overcoats. Cold wind blows rubbish and newspapers. Red, white, and blue Fords, Chevys, and Buicks go by, and Yellow Cabs unload in front. Stars and Stripes flap in full extension, on a 30-foot pole, above Southern's Birmingham headquarters.

How anyone might predict or prepare for a turn of fortune and twist of fate such as this Gerry fails to comprehend. For three weeks since November 25, little else has mattered. For two days of testimony, she feels as if she viewed a parade of faces and lives altered, in some cases, for a lifetime and, for others, a short while. What's the difference, she wonders, how one way and why another —an age-old question.

At 4:00, Mr. Shults calls things to order a last time. He reads his notes and recaps, "Thus far, we've talked to participants as we have been able. Yesterday, we talked to Conductors Sullivan of Second 47 and Hoadley of 48. Unfortunately, some crew members are unable to be heard. Those matters lie beyond our control— beyond scope of this meeting. Today, we talked to Alass from 48 and Second 47's Engineer Mr. Love."

Outside, through the still crowded hallway, a next witness moves slow, his back in a burdensome brace, up to the back of his head. His forehead looks spotted and marked with dispersed red dots—sores—as if he received a close round of buckshot. His arms are bandaged but free, he wears street clothes, brown slacks, white cotton dress shirt, and tan oxford shoes. His curly hair hangs a bit long but his face shaven for most part—between dots, spots, and scabs. People wish him well and shake his hand, a warm reception in every way. He enjoys his first day out of Druid City Hospital in almost three weeks. They predicted his stay a month, if all went well.

Shults asks, "Is Fireman Gambrell out there?"

As soon as Shults's question clears his mouth, Robert enters— slow and steady, unsmiling, but without grimace or pain or tear— free of surprise and wonder.

He looks good, better than Gerry has seen since before wreck.

He walks to front of hearing room, and Ms. Hale accompanies him to his seat. Mr. Clark inhales a deep last breath and begins again, "Mr. Gambrell, records show that you were born on October 17, 1918, and that you entered the service of the Alabama Great Southern Railroad Company as a fireman on January 10, 1946, and that you were promoted to locomotive engineer on March 25, 1946. That is correct, is it not?"

"Yes, sir."

Clark remains seated, covering preliminaries and general questions a last time, before getting serious, "About what speed was your train being operated passing Signal 1699 at Green Pond, the last signal before North Switch at Woodstock?"

"We were going about 71 or 72 miles per hour, I would say to the best of my knowledge and remembrance."

"Where were you riding?"

"In the left seat, on the fireman's seat."

"Were you in a position to observe the speedometer?"

"I could observe it by leaning a little bit in my seat towards the engineer's side," to which he draws another muffled relief chuckle from somewhere in back.

"Mr. Pape was occupying the center seat, and Mr. Love was operating the engine?"

"Yes, sir."

"And the signal at Green Pond, was displaying a proceed signal when Second 47 passed?"

"Yes, sir."

"And you did call the indication to the engineer?"

"Yes, sir."

"In your own words, Mr. Gambrell, state what took place between 1699 at Green Pond and the North Switch at Woodstock where the collision occurred."

"Of course, when we passed the clear signal, there was no reduction in the speed. And, when we came to the top of the hill and around the curve, where the engineer usually notches down throttle off two or three notches, because it is going to be downgrade, Mr. Pape, sitting in the middle seat, jumped up and said, 'My God, he's on the mainline.' His seat is a little higher than mine, so I jumped up too. By that time, we had gotten fairly close to 48, so I looked at it all, just came to me in a flash. As I looked out, I could see the fireman trying to wave us down, and as I turned back around, why, he was gone. Mr. Pape had disappeared. So, I walked over. It came to me in a flash. We were in the right curve, so I walked to that side of the engine and climbed down the footsteps to the bottom rung and waited until we got as close to 48 as I thought we could. I waited as long as possible before I jumped. Like I say, it was a flash. After that, I don't remember anything until late that night at Druid City Hospital."

Clark draws on his pad with a pen in a mindless way, his face solemn, "You did know when you jumped from the engine that a collision was going to occur?"

Robert interlocks his fingers near his stomach, "Yes, sir, I knew it was inevitable. I held on as long as I could before I did jump."

"In your opinion, how far was Second 47 from the North Switch at Woodstock, from 48, when Mr. Pape stated he thought 48 was on the main track?"

"I don't know exactly. I know we were already going to the right pretty sharp. I would say at least maybe three train lengths. I wouldn't be sure on that."

"Did you yourself see Fireman Alass attempting to flag down your train, Second 47?"

"Yes, sir. I saw him myself."

"When you left the engine from the engineer's side, the brakes had at that time been applied in emergency?"

"Yes, sir."

"Had the speed of your train, Second 47, been materially reduced when you left the engine?"

"It seemed that it had, yes, sir."

"Could you give us any estimate as to how much your train's speed had been reduced when you jumped?"

"That is kind of hard to say. I was just hanging down there in the wind. No way to judge. I was watching the trestle. I would say it had been reduced from whatever speed we were going maybe 15 or 20 miles an hour. Just an estimate, of course. But it had to be reduced some. I had that in mind to hang on as long as I could, so it would slow down more."

"And you alighted from the engine at about four car lengths, or 200 feet, from 48's engine?"

"Yes, sir. The other side of that little trestle. Don't know just how 48's engine stood in regard to that trestle, but I know I jumped off before I got to the trestle."

"Did you see 48's engineer, Engineer Pyler, before the collision?"

"I didn't know it at the time, but it must have been him. Someone stuck his head out of the phone booth by the train, by 48, and looked at our engine about time I was ready to leave the engine."

"You assume that was Mr. Pyler?"

"Yes, sir."

Clark rests again, and Mr. Dansforth asks, "When Mr. Pape said that he believed 48 was on the main track, was any action taken by Mr. Love at that time?"

"Whether Mr. Love put the brake on in emergency right then, I really don't know. I jumped up to see for myself and made my own arrangements. Whether Cecil waited until he saw for himself, I don't know. He might have hesitated to be sure." Robert touches his left shirt pocket, his Sir Walter Raleigh, his hand as always quaking—ever so light.

Dansforth looks at a couple of sheets and tosses them aside. "Did Road Foreman of Engines Pape tell you to jump or warn you to get off before he left?"

"No, sir, he didn't."

"I believe you said that you jumped from the lowest rung of the ladder on the right side of the locomotive. Is that right?"

"Yes, sir."

"And you were injured?"

"Broken back."

"Anything else?"

Robert lifts both his arms, turns his palms skyward, showing dozens of dots and spots from cinders and fragments, his face discolored, and each arm sporting bandages. He shrugs a little.

Dansforth, glances to Shults and Clark, and carries on, "And, you don't remember, you were evidently knocked unconscious by the impact, you don't remember anything after that?"

"No, sir."

Five people occupied cabs going into Woodstock. Engineer J. D. Pyler of stranded northbound 48 died while at a trackside phone calling to report situation and seek help, wreckage covered him as it spread. Road Foreman Sam Pape after shouting, "My God, he's on the mainline", went immediately to Second 47's lead engine's right-side door and jumped. He was killed on landing. Cecil lost his hand inside cab. Robert for whatever reason crossed cab, waited as long as he could on lowest rung of ladder, leaped, broke his back, and obtained permanent scratches and marks caused by cinder, ashes, and gravel. Forty-eight's Fireman C. R. Alass ran up track waving an orange rag and lived. Fifteen passengers died and 66 received serious injury. Everyone's best laid plan went astray indeed.

9

Cottage 'Neath Live Oak Tree

Robert's references to one of two favorite poems describes a soldier after battle envisioning, as if by wand of fairy, a cottage 'neath the live oak tree and his loved ones standing before him— among other things. He seldom if ever underestimates significance and appropriateness of endless quotes and quips.

He comes home once testimony at Southern's office building completed, Woodstock and Druid City Hospital now battlefields in his rearview. He creeps and suffers in brace and mostly wants to lie down. Yet, he made it home alive, quite a trip and feat. For a second time, he brushed death—so close it raised hairs on his raw arms— surviving by his whiskers which began to grow long. His Iwo Jima war days fade away more and more, Second 47's demise might. He thinks little gratifies and glorifies life as death.

Gerry helps, facing challenges of her own—being his unenviable nurse and their much-needed bread winner, two of many. Life changes forever.

Friends ring his phone often, but for a while, a faster spinning world stays at bay, allowing reestablishment. He becomes quieter again and his bodily movement shows little improvement. Real world months go by in his absence, him at home, little to do except be trapped and restless. Robert's robust personality requires expanse, enrichment, and stimulation. His mind goes back to Dinah at the station and her legs, a ticket out and away. Around house, when Gerry goes to town or work, he resorts to singing, Someone in the kitchen with Dinah and Fee-fi-fiddly-eye-o, fee-fi-fiddly-eye-o-o-o. He lacks voice making his Dinah longing worse.

Gerry gets itchy too, having him underfoot—long face and dragging rump—and he still possesses ability to needle and tease and downright annoy as he wishes and often does.

Something has to give.

Winter crawls and spring helps less than ever and summer simmers Down South. By August, she has enough, "Well, I've asked them all over, for Labor Day. We'll start early and have a cookout or cook in, as weather allows, and they can all come and go however they like." She walks over and looks into imprisoned eyes and continues, "We'll ask as many people as will come."

Without moving, he studies her. He takes both hands and tries to better his sickbed or depressed sprawl, "We can't afford to do all that. We're behind on bills now." He begins to roll over but surrenders, "Hell, we'll be ruined."

"Well, they're coming, and we're going to meet them, and Buster's going to finish our house, and you're going back to work. That simple. We'll worry about the railroad later."

Robert stares down at his sheets, rearranges them—almost noon. "Damnation." He contemplates and in time looks up at Gerry, "A new dawn awaits."

Luckily for both, except for final touches, their house has reached completion, livable and cozy but real warm, air conditioning still uncommon in early 1950's. Their five or so acres of lawn, field, and woods offers aesthetic and natural relief, diversion, and shade of overhanging pine, dogwood, mimosa, and red and white oak—rather than poet Thompson's live oak, dominating nearer Gulf of Mexico.

On Labor Day impulse, Robert says to hell with it. Free from brace—tossed in closet—he grabs swing blade and shears and begins to cut anything resembling leafage—grown over from summer— bushes, twigs, vines, saplings, anything in his path. Buster, who comes up early weekends and holidays to finish his odd job list, chips in by picking up and stacking fallen vegetation, creating brush piles in Robert's erratic swath. Buster and Gerry both know, when Robert gets a bend on—look out.

Gerry begins grilling meat, taking time to squint at Robert's industrious and dubious endeavors. After a long watch, Buster becomes doubter, wipes hands, scratches his head, abandons Robert and joins Gerry's cooking—something with clear and identifiable objectives and results. Gerry stands taller than Buster. He wears his half gray hair full and thick around round rimless spectacles. He smiles often, cheerful and unaffected by underlying agenda. Buster inheres blessed old-fashioned simplicity and precious lack of complication.

All three, especially Robert, relish their outside holiday activity and yardwork, but it's dang hot. Early September only hints cooler weather so far south.

Wilder Barnes, conductor and dear friend, arrives first. An attendee and minor participant, as union rep, throughout NTSB's hearings, he understands The Wreck's elements, intricacies, complications, and results as well as anyone. Wilder, also a WWII marine, shares Robert's zest for life, humor, intelligence, and, most of all and especially under influence, poetic nature and aspiration. Of all Robert's friends, only Wilder can match him or even come close on literature, history, and quick thinking afoot. He shares Robert's fondness for Jack Daniel's, in shots and quantity. When Wilder and Robert unite, eloquence and classical—and unclassical—reference abounds and flows.

Wilder wheels his spotless, box shaped, '51, jade sedan into driveway. Plymouths look much like Chevys and Fords, perhaps squarer and more conservative, enough head room for hat wearing. Wilder sports wide white walls, he gases a little, listens and shuts her down. People love cars as much as gadgets, having so little of them growing up. They arrive in style.

Gerry and Buster turn meat and smoke billows. She admires Wilder's intellect, wit, and character.

Wilder gets out and stands motionless. He winks at Buster and Gerry and puts his finger to his lips as if to say don't let Robert know I'm here. He lowers his impish brows and considers Robert's arduous land clearing. He puts hands on hips and radiates, sustaining scrutiny, only an occasional glance toward Gerry and Willow Lane's wood and field. Robert prolongs his narrow improvements, unaware anyone else in world exists, unable to hear anything other than his own chopping, cutting, and heavy panting. Wilder evaluates and marvels—two poetic souls nabbed in nature's vast web. At last, Robert has enough, he picks up his swing blade, wipes a white hanky across his sopping brow, and turns around. He appears surprised and quizzical to see Wilder already there and watching.

Wilder has an actor's love for being on cue and embraces theatrical allusion and emulation. He raises his right hand and index finger straight up a few inches above head, breathes deep, tightens his diaphragm, and speaks in his precise and clear, maybe a little high-pitched stage voice, "Ah, felling the forest." Robert stands speechless.

Gerry shouts, "Wilder," and trots to hug him.

As always, Wilder maintains poise—his manners impeccable and use of language fluid. A Virginian, from Arlington—DC—at impressionable ages, he acts more politician or teacher than working man. His frame shows a trim waistline, putting him in minority on the '50's version of the Alabama Great Southern Railroad.

"He's doing better," as he inspects Robert still standing in thicket. Wilder's voice exudes sensitivity. Some might, by mistake, call it effeminate.

Robert swells with pride before his friend—morning toils near completion but first he sets fire to Buster's little slash piles of felled vegetation. He watches them glow and smoke but, being so green and fresh, they fizzle for most part.

Wilder clasps hands in front of himself and drums fingers tips in light tapping bounces, as Robert sometimes does. He, business casual, watches Robert, resurrected man of people, come closer. Wilder has reddish brown hair, every short strand in place. They shake hands and embrace. "You're doing well, my wounded warrior friend," Wilder tells him. "Indeed, you are. And you fared well at your hearings. I was there, if you didn't notice me, your wits still asunder. You may not have been aware of my ever-watchful presence," almost satirical, as he and Robert always go.

Robert surveys Wilder's face—bright, astute, with shining, piercing, kind, delighted eyes. "Wilder, this has been one hell of an ordeal."

"I know it, Robert. Lucky for you, you have Geraldine and family and friends who support and think of you."

Buster barbecues ribs, chicken, burgers, and dogs.

"Oh, excuse me, Wilder, this is Buster Powell." Buster comes over to shake. "He is a friend—lives a few houses down Willow Lane here. You passed his house coming in. He's been helping me build—rather he built—this house—cottage—one step at a time. And soon, we complete it. Right Buster? I'm afraid Buster's been doing it mostly on his own, I haven't been much help."

Congenial Wilder shakes Buster's hand, "Good day to you, Buster, a friend of Robert's is a friend of mine. Robert it's understandable you've had to depend on Buster considering your condition and all you've been through. You two will get it done, my friends." And, with his sharp grin, "You'll get it done as sure as morning brings light, summer brings growth, autumn harvest, winter another year, and spring love to man's heart—and body."

Robert shakes his head still a bit discolored and sprinkled with healing sores. Buying in, he almost laughs, but moans and agrees, "Wilder," a timely pause, "you bring truth—and good tidings. I expect no less."

Wilder gives Gerry a once or twice over as he stands by their smoking red hot grill and thinks she sure looks heavy but for once, he remains quiet.

They all stand looking around and through Buster and Gerry's smoke at woods and trees and field—an excellent day to relax, enjoy, party, forget, and look forward.

Standing nearby listening and observing Gerry catches a third discreet inspection from Wilder. She steps over closer to their circle—Robert, Wilder, and Buster.

She leans toward Wilder as if to curtsy but stops and announces so all three can hear, "Yes, Wilder, I'm expecting."

If Buster knew or saw before, he failed to show it. Wilder looks surprised, almost shaken, "Geraldine, this is wonderful news. I am most happy for you and Robert. I didn't know."

Robert confirms with little facial expression and in monotone, "'Tis true."

Agnew Dillard "Frank" Sparks arrives and joins them, one of a few encounters with Robert since November 25, when he and C. W. Cottrell came in on 17 from Chattanooga and conversed with departing Robert at station before his mounting doomed Second 47.

Robert calls his given name, "Agnew," and shakes Sparks's hand. "You know all these people? Where is Helen?"

"She won't be coming, Bob. She's got things going on with the boy. She said tell y'all she's sorry but school's coming, you know. We'll have y'all over sometime." Sparks nods at welcoming Gerry. They've all been friends a long time. Sparks remains much quieter and less flamboyant than Wilder and Robert, but any wise unsuspecting soul must understand, he has far more than ample good sense, personality, and morals.

One by one Robert, Wilder, and Sparks osmose through a side screen entrance into cottage kitchen. Robert pulls three fifths of Jack Daniel's Old No. 7, green label, from a white metal kitchen cabinet. Wilder and Sparks ease closer, forming a shrinking semicircle. Robert replaces two fifths on shelf and plops one bottle of "Jack" on his linoleum counter.

As if magical and clairvoyant, R. E. "Red" Duncan enters as if beckoned, in an unmistakable, patented, and noisy barrage. Red knows little if anything of silence, restraint, and reticence. Quite different from his cohorts, he dresses in chocolate brown polyester pants, white Hawaiian shirt with large green palm trees and bluish hula dancers, and bright red rayon scarf. His gold chain and medallion hang from neck. He removes his Australian ranch hat—displaying his bald, glowing, pink head—and places on counter. One thing, and maybe only one, Red shares with many of his fellow railroaders: an inflated and protruding stomach, a result of a new-found good life.

"Red, where the hell you been?" Robert acts as if he hasn't seen Red or any of these people in months though he has. They all came to visit him in Druid City Hospital, it doesn't count. And most visited time to time here at home in his convalescence but things are different now—much different. Red and Wilder hold local union positions and attended all public hearings regarding wreck, but again those days feel lifetimes away.

Sparks and Wilder like Red too. He misleads, but once you know him, Red proves honest, straightforward, and tender. Gerry contends, he has a good heart—and brain. They all shake hands and slap shoulders.

Robert tries again, "Where you been, Red?"

"I'm right c'here!" with a loud laugh. He's all oversized ears and predominate teeth.

Robert asks, "Where's Dolly-o?" speaking of Red's wife.

Red speaks in a deep, gravelly, scratchy voice, forming truncated, friendly growls in short, warm spurts—most unusual combinations, "Her beautiful self—is outside talking to Geraldine—and that little guy from down the street."

Robert says, "Buster."

"Yep, him." Red surveys his friends and communion. "Did you see The Leg Spreader, Bob?"

"I saw you pass by the window and turn in the drive—quite an entrance."

Robert has seen Red's new crimson Caddie convertible, one of quite a few he's owned. As Robert and local railroaders know, Red's fancy autos accentuate his character and perpetuate his fame up and down the line.

Robert grabs Jack and begins pouring shots into four six-ounce Bama brand jelly jars. "Well, this calls for a drink."

Red, as Wilder earlier, comments, "I sure didn't know about Geraldine."

Robert replies again, "'Tis true." He picks up his glass eye level and inspects contents.

Red a bit lost for words, "She's expecting."

"I didn't know either," Sparks joins. "Big surprise."

Wilder raises his glass, "I propose a toast, a most deserved one—to Robert and Geraldine and their baby."

Sparks, "Hear! Hear!" and Red, "'At a boy."

After a pause, Wilder asks, "How far along is she?"

Robert answers, "Six months."

Sparks rolls his eyes a brief second and lifts his Bama glass, and as driest of all in attendance, says to Red, "Well, Bob wasn't hurt too bad."

Red figures in silence, Robert tightens his lips.

Wilder toasts, "Robert and Geraldine!"

All friends gather closer, each playing his role: Robert, host protagonist; Sparks, faithful servant of people, job, and life; Wilder, a diamond in rough; and Red, let chips fall wherever they may.

Robert pours another Jack for each and raises his glass to lead, but Sparks interrupts, "Hold on, Bob, hold on," wrapping his hand around glass, "let me make it." He contemplates, "Let's make a toast to 1952, a very good year."

Wilder—bard and poet laureate—chimes in, "Nineteen hundred and fifty-two is an outstanding year—free of pestilence, disease, war—excepting one—and hardship. It is a time for celebration of life and death."

They all raise their glass.

Wilder endures, "This time, like all times, is a good one, if we only know but what to do with it."

"Who said?" Robert asks, face a little wry.

"Emerson," Wilder speaks in confidence, "a little on rough side."

They all three set their glasses down and concur in general, "Damn good year."

Robert pours.

Kids rush through from outside. Sounds filter in from patio—laughter and music playing.

Robert raises glass, his eyes seek and search Wilder for new topic.

"I yield to you, my dear friend," Wilder counters. "'The most I can do for my friend is simply be his friend.'"

Robert glances up into thin air at ceiling, "Who?"

Wilder responds, "Thoreau."

They all begin to drink, but Robert halts them, "Whoa, boys, let me do my toast." He studies until Red pronounces, "To Second 47."

They swallow hard, as big as before.

Wilder takes front and center, "Robert, you know, Red and I sat through those entire Safety Board meetings, from uninformed beginning to clarified conclusion. What do you think happened?"

Robert pauses and in a somber tone, "I don't think we'll ever know for sure. We'll never be certain."

Sparks spins his glass and calculates, "I listened to it all too and talked to a lot of people all over the railroad. Engineer—Old Man—Pyler and Fireman Alass, on 48, just misread their signal. And it looks like they were going fast through the siding too. I wonder how much or if they even tried to slow or stop until it was too late."

Wilder goes on, "Or for whatever reason, they were distracted or inattentive. There is no other conclusion. There is no other plausible assertion, my friends."

Red injects, his voice even raspier from fresh Tennessee whiskey, "That's right. Y'all absolutely got it. The damned ole railroad and government did studies of the signal and tracks and engines and brake time and weather and lighting. You name it, they studied it. Old Man Pyler and that dumbass Alass just fouled it all up. That's all there is to it. No two ways about it."

Robert weighs his friends' contentions. For some reason, through it all, he's avoided assumptions, conclusions, and has failed to lay blame, but now, he wonders more than ever. "I've had a great deal of time to think it all over. I don't think we'll ever know what happened." He throws his hands out, "We'll never know for sure what they did—what they saw. We do have a good idea what they didn't do."

Sparks asserts, "We're right, Bob. There ain't no one up and down the railroad who disagrees with what Wilder, Red, and I are saying."

Red informs their group, "I just heard yesterday, the Southern fired Alass for a number of mistakes he and Old Man Pyler made on 48. He'll never work again on this or any railroad. And that's the way it should be. He's a good ole boy, I guess, but we're all out there, up and down the line. There's no room for that kind of carelessness and errors. And Pyler sure won't work any damn where either. And that's the way it should be too. All the wreckage just spread out and went all over him. He may have seen it coming but he didn't really know or feel what the heck hit him. Dead as a door nail." Red picks up his empty glass, looks at it, and sets her down. "I'm going out back to find ole Dolly-o." Red turns and starts toward door, patio, and party. Music plays outside intermingled with more and more voices, chatter, and revelry.

Sparks stops him, "Red, did you hear what Uncle Cecil's saying? He's telling everybody he told Bob to jump. He says he said jump, boy, jump. Is that right, Bob? Did he tell you that?"

All three look to Robert.

Sparks asks again, "Did he say that?"

Robert delays first then states, "No—he didn't say anything at all."

Sparks asks, "Why not, you think?"

Robert places his hand on Gerry's counter, by her sink, her set of copper flour, sugar, coffee, and tea canisters.

"Too scared. We were all too scared to say anything."

They all grow quiet, each thinking, rubbing his chin, or scratching. Red reinitiates his exit and remarks, "I knew ole Cecil was full of it on that one." He heads for door but remembers, "Oh, I found this." He holds out a sheet of rolled up paper and flips it down restating, "I gotta go out here and see how Dolly-o and the gals are getting along." He heads for door singing and humming, Fee-fi-fiddly-eye-o, fee-fi-fiddly-eye-o-o-o.

Robert wonders if Red and others realize where Dinah and her verses, tunes, and allusions come from.

He, as most, see Red as an enigma among railroad people in era of traditional values mixed with home-spun good ole boy antics. His core may wander little from his contemporaries, his background he keeps to himself, avoiding outside inspection, how-ever, somewhere and somehow along the line, Red shrouds himself in a flashy, glittery, showy exterior unlike any chronicled by local railroad history, scuttlebutt, or folklore. Yet, outlandish as many find him, his undiminished character, popularity, and status thrives. He's a damned good engineer too, ask anyone.

Three remaining drinkers feel their sauce. Wilder unrolls Red's document for Robert and Sparks to inspect, "Yes, I have a copy of this. It was distributed at Safety Board meetings." He raises one finger again as if to say hark, "I have reviewed it." He spreads it flat on counter and holds it open.

Exhibit #16
Transcript of personal record of J. D. Pyler, Engineer, No. 48
Date of Birth   November 27, 1882
9-14-1907   Entered service as Engineer
5-3-1921   30 demerits account Train 68, overlooked
order on No. 51 at Boligee
2-28-1923   30 demerits for concern in accident between
Train 65 and Extra 6583, Tuscaloosa, Train 65 running
through switch
10-1-1934   20 demerits for responsibility in connection
with accident Train 66, Tuscaloosa

Wilder remains quiet, exhibit still displayed.

Robert reasons, "That doesn't mean a thing, not a thing really. There's a lot of that out there." He walks to his back door, where Red exited, and sizes his growing party.

"I don't know, Bob." Sparks looks concerned. "I mean, mistakes and violations and demerits are one thing, but accidents, especially with other trains, are another. Most don't have any of those. Not a bad one." He grimaces, "If you do, it's a one in a lifetime deal—usually."

Wilder closes document, "History repeats itself."

Robert shakes it all off or tries, "I don't know. It doesn't matter now. It doesn't matter anymore," but thinks and wonders, "Wilder, you've heard all the interviews. What exactly did happen to Old Man Pyler?"

Wilder recounts, enjoying centerstage significance, as if soliloquizing, "Pyler and Alass split up after getting down from stranded 48's engine." He pauses, his hands and arms in wide sweeping motions as if pointing across a field—a scene or a stage, "As you know, Alass ran ahead to flag down you and Cecil on Second 47. Pyler went back to a little emergency phone by the tracks, just behind 48's engine, to call for help—dispatcher, I presume."

Robert whispers, "So I did see someone in a phone booth. I knew I did. As I thought, it was Old Man Pyler sticking his head out—peering."

"Yes, it was he," Wilder sums and bows his head. "Mr. Pyler met his destiny—his maker—while trying to call from a trackside phone booth—a futile cry for help for fate's deaf ears." Wilder feigns smashing his hands, clenched fists, together, "When the two engines collided, 48's engine shot backwards 50 or 60 feet, by some accounts to which official record agrees. All the engines and baggage cars spread out in the crash, from the impact. It simply engulfed Pyler and his phone booth." Wilder grows more courteous, "It took them a long time to find him. He was one of the last to be located—at the bottom of the wreckage."

"Dead as a doornail," Sparks sums. "It's a wonder all you on those engines weren't killed—a true wonder."

Robert frowns, standing and appearing statuesque, "And Pape? Anything new about him?"

Wilder answers, "Yes, Mr. Pape died instantly. He jumped from the top, didn't he?"

Robert replies, "He did, I assume—he was gone in an instant. I turned around and as I said at the hearing, 'Why, he was gone.'"

"He jumped from top. He went straight to door and jumped," Wilder knows from all official accounts.

Sparks, deep in thought, gives his empty glass mindless thumps, "Robert, good thing you climbed down to the bottom of the ladder. Good—or lucky—you didn't just jump. Word is you're dead if you did."

"That's what the docs told me. Going down the ladder and waiting before jumping saved me, reduced speed and height—and impact."

"Good thing," Sparks pushes his empty glass to center of counter.

Wilder asks, "Robert, what inspired you?"

Robert pours a last for a while, "I don't know. It just came in a flash, in an instant, like I said in testimony. Everything happened so fast but, at the same time, everything slowed down—to a crawl. You could see everything at once and hear everything, every single sound." He rubs his finger around his glass's top.

Sparks says, "I do have one question though. What became of ole Skitts? You told me and C. W. that day at the station, the day of the wreck, you saw him, and he was gonna be on your train taking it all the way to New Orleans. But I was down at the Southern's employee building the other day, and they've got a story about the wreck and official numbers posted: 18 dead, 70 seriously injured. And there's a list of names, but no one mentions or seems to have heard of ole Skitts." Sparks tilts his glass, getting every last bronze colored drop. "I even looked at the conductor's passenger and crew lists and no Skitts mentioned anywhere. It's like he didn't exist. So, I haven't even got an idea. Was he even on the train? There's a lot of mystery."

"I did see him at the station, just like I said." Robert remembers, "But, there's been such upheaval. I haven't thought much of anybody other than myself—and Cecil—and, of course, Pape. I don't know. Geraldine's kept all the newspapers since the wreck 'til now. She'll look back and see. I don't know. Skitts evades me. Of course, he may have been riding in the Coloreds that time of afternoon—they were hit."

Sparks concedes, "I don't understand it all."

"Me either." Robert feels wasted.

Wilder picks up, "I don't know Skitts. I never worked with him on the north end, but the third car on each train, the first coach, took the heaviest jolt, force, and casualties. The third—the

Colored—car on 48 telescoped, and on Second 47, the third car—the Coloreds—went down into the mining train underpass. Coloreds took biggest hit, undoubtedly, on both trains."

Three glasses bang on counter. Robert advising, "Gentlemen, we must adjourn out of doors."

Sparks says, "Well, Pape, didn't."

Robert asks, "Didn't what?"

"Didn't see it all in a flash, in an instant. He jumped from top step and died."

Wilder empathizes, "Someone must die. Someone."

Robert winces, "Shakespeare?"

Wilder glows, eyes afire, tilting his head as if unknowing, "Someone said it. I'm unsure who at present moment but someone. Let's join merriment and frivolity."

Outside, Robert pats drinking buddies on back, and they venture and mingle as kids going out to play. Gerry carries a tray of barbecue condiments and seizes brief opportunity to mollify, "Robert, now use some moderation. You can still have a good time without getting all—stoned faced—" She stops and reconsiders. Judging from his tilted stance and leaning stagger, it's too late.

Gerry's brother's RCA Victor spins 78 RPM's: big bands, little orchestra, crooners, and country. Everyone brought discs and dancing prevails—Charleston to Jitterbug to boogie to square dance, line, clog, waltz, fox trot, and tango.

Red loves to dance, "Come on, Ger'dine, lets dip." He throws his arms around her, and his big feet begin to stomp and scrape on concrete. "Dolly-o don't mind, do you, Dolly-o!" Gerry stood with Dolly-o Duncan, Red's wife., and Lucille Cottrell, C. W.'s spouse and Gerry's lifelong friend who introduced her to Robert. Brad and Charles, Robert's brothers, and their wives gather close by. Everyone who's anyone in local railroad circles attends as do neighbors and other friends and acquaintances. They dance into darkness.

Gerry laughs, "Oh, Red—" After a step or two, she tries to free her arms to push him off, but his chunky arms move up and slide down, again pinning her arms at her sides. His big gut bounces off her protruding motherly belly.

She tries to explain, I can't dip, I'm expecting. He tightens and puts his nose close to her face, "Come on, Ger'dine, we'll show 'em how it's done." And off they go, like it or not. He spins and twirls and keeps pounding his large feet—clad in slick, smooth, reflecting two-tone tan and white alligator saddle oxfords with golden strings. They sweep all around to every corner, by condiment table, in front of curious ladies and gentlemen alike. They dip right past Cecil, Conductor Sullivan, and their wives who Gerry hasn't seen since hearings. She wants to tell them all, everyone in attendance, Actually, the expecting lady's just trying to catch her breath.

"Red, I need air." She smiles but twists and turns. On next revolution, to her relief, Red fatigues. As a bear toying his prey, he releases her to her group right where their struggle began. Everyone figures Red for dead, but when Patti Page starts singing Tennessee Waltz, he wants more and shouts, "Come on, Dolly-o." All ladies agree, Better her than me, and true what they say, For every man there is somewhere a woman.

Dolly-o wears her hair big, frazzled, and scorched—overdone, harsh, and unprofessional. Her clothes hang—gaudy and revealing —her attitude devil-may-care. Yet, for Dolly-o and ole Red, it all comes together. Little accentuates enigma as enigma. One strong taste offsets another, making each more palatable. Everyone shares love for the Duncan's—Red and Dolly-o.

Song after song play into late afternoon, dance after dance embrace each couple. Any neighbors, who by choice fail to attend, hear but what the hey, so little happens on Willow Lane and its little cottage 'neath live oak tree. Let them swing a little, blow it out.

Everyone feasts and disperses as night falls on Birmingham, Alabama. Gerry puts away what little perishables remain and goes a long line toward bed leaving Robert, Sparks, and overnight guest Wilder with it. How much drink they consumed, as always, remains in question, and as usual about this time, exhaustion and euphoria, or drunken stupor, descend, and they begin to hum and sway to their fave, "The Blue Danube Waltz". Gerry, walking down hall, sizes them up, as if they're from outer space, and shakes her head. They lock arms and caterwaul—red noses glowing, sinuses blowing as heralding trumpets, and tears falling as sobering and healing, gentle rain from Heaven.

Wilder visits classics and greats from Melville to Longfellow to Poe and Yeats.

Sparks listens, laughs, and hums along. He asks Robert what his favorite poems are. Robert sits for a second, for politeness and effect, and answers with little doubt using his hands for emphasis, "'Invictus', penned by Henley—the gods, and 'Music in Camp', by Thompson—Civil War reflections."

Conversation begins to slow. Sparks digs further, enjoying it all, "And Invictus means—?"

"Unconquerable."

"Yes, that's absolutely right," Wilder waves a hand. "Get up, Robert, get up. Please do 'Invictus'. Do it all. Few others make Henley so proud."

Robert totters and gleams.

Their phone interrupts in groups of two long rings—his despised party-line signal. He hears it first, flinches, and yanks head around. Unfazed, Wilder and Sparks chatter more about authors and rhyme and song. Gerry, almost unheard below talk, music, and singing, says, "I'll get it," and comes from other room to central entrance hall. "Hello."

Helen Sparks asks from line's other end—almost as if asking a stranger—brief, direct, loud, clear, cold, sharp, nasally enunciated, and uncaring of party line status, "Is Frank Sparks there?"

Gerry replies, "Yes, he is," as pleasant, singsong, and unrevealing of current party status as possible.

"This is Helen Sparks, his wife. Will you tell him, I said, to get his ass home."

Gerry likes Helen a lot and says in a polite way, "You better tell him." She sets down receiver, "Frank, it's for you."

Sparks—eyes bloodshot and wet, nose runny and aglow—fresh off quoting Keats and working on Kipling, takes his call. After a couple of seconds, he hangs up. In about ten more, he excuses himself and leaves without explanation, formality, or fanfare. For one, Helen, as nice as can be, might outweigh him a bit, and secondly, she isn't in a Keats or Kipling state of mind or mood.

With Sparks's and their guests' sudden exodus, Robert and Wilder talk into wee hours. As he lies down on couch, resting his head on throw pillow, Wilder says, "'A woman's guess is much more accurate than a man's certainty.'"

Robert, still enthralled, "Who?"

"Rudyard Kipling." Wilder, almost dozing, rolls on, "'When you are wounded and left on Afghanistan's plains, and the women come out to cut up what remains, just roll to your rifle and blow out your brains and go to your god like a soldier.'"

Robert prods, "Rudyard?"

"Indeed, dear friend, indeed." Wilder sleeps.

Robert looks around his "cottage" living room and out into scattered streetlight on late summer Willow Lane where November 25, 1951, dawned—a lifetime—before. He measures Wilder and himself and for some reason almost feels sorry for each.

Just before surrendering and retiring, Robert hears sirens and sees flashing red lights in his windows. At his door, a lone fireman tells him rising wind spread fire from a smoldering leaf pile, he lit earlier in day, across dry, previously cut grasses into his neighbors' yards, one of a number of times, through years, distracted Robert's wildfires scorched Mother Earth.

After firemen leave, he peeks in toward his bedstead and wife and hears her alarm clock ticking and her breathing. If she heard commotion, she fails to show it.

He goes back to check and look down on peaceful Wilder sleeping undisturbed and unaware.

He wraps himself in quotations—as a beggar would enfold himself in purple of Emperors. And thinks, Kipling.

10

Caboose

Out of the night that covers me
Black as a pit from pole to pole
I thank whatever gods may be
For my unconquerable soul
--from Invictus, Henley

Late fall came to Birmingham and Willow Lane and on November 13, Gerry gave Robert and herself a third son.

Robert continued to negotiate an agreement and return to work. At last, in late 1952, over a year after The Wreck, he settled for $15,000 less lawyer fees, court costs, and miscellaneous medical and living expenses incurred over a year's disability. Gerry thanked Lord and everyone for help and support during a long year with only her meager income, and—as she did her entire life—exalted, "Railroad people, there ain't nothing like 'em."

After 14 months, Robert fired an engine again in early 1953, what a relief. Several months later he became Local Chairman for his Union, the Brotherhood of Locomotive Firemen and Enginemen. He began to enter his niche, find his calling. His speaking, reasoning ability, quick brain, and people skills took him in a direction he needed to go. Things went well for a long time.

In December 1959, the Southern ran a Liberty Bowl Special—an entire party train for a football cause—from Birmingham to Philadelphia. Passengers included Robert and his three sons. Philly's old Municipal Stadium turned frigid and windy for Liberty Bowl's inaugural game, and Bear Bryant's first of 24 consecutive bowl games as Alabama coach. Penn State won 7-0 on a fake field goal TD thrown by Galen Hall, future Florida and PSU coach—exciting stuff. A couple of days later, the Liberty Bowl Special pulled back into Birmingham's Terminal Station, more than a few riders somehow convinced Jack Daniel's drinking Robert might run for governor. Rumor had it Governor Jim Folsom, a renowned drinker, spent much of his time passed out in last car, reserved for dignitaries. Booze flowed freely throughout a disorderly trip—unintended and unfit for meek.

A few months later, Robert and Gerry moved family across Birmingham from Willow Lane to Red Mountain—a city view and more perspective.

In 1961, Robert took his eight-year-old and same age friend aboard engine on a ride on Southern's 41, *The Pelican*, Birmingham to Meridian, he as fireman and Red Duncan engineer. We rode thru Woodstock, same sights and stops as Robert, Pape, and Cecil enjoyed a decade before on doomed Second 47. I can still see Red's thick paws moving brake and throttle, hear him growl and roar loud above his diesel engine, remember how 41's light shone down lonely Alabama and Mississippi tracks. In Meridian, we rested and dined at Union Hotel—just like railroad men. Boarding 48's engine to take us back to Birmingham we climbed a ladder, as Robert used to detrain seconds before his Woodstock's collision a decade before. We ate baloney and crackers as if crew and pulled on whistle cord when instructed by Fireman Gambrell or Engineer Duncan.

Things were different then, a boy on his father's engine—riding a steel magic carpet. Steve Goodman wrote about something similar in "City of New Orleans." John Prine called Goodman's tune, greatest train song he ever heard—tall cotton. Arlo Guthrie sang it; Willie Nelson covered it.

I recall being stopped on sidetrack, somewhere in Mississippi, urinating from engine door, probably 10 to 12 feet above ground. A young black kid, doing same, watched from bushes, a thicket behind a slag pile. We scrutinized each other a long while, both curious of other, until 48's whistle blasted a couple of times and northbound wheels began to roll.

Red and Robert contrived international brainstorms. They heard and read announcements for qualified locomotive enginemen to tutor people on working railroad—in Liberia. In spring 1962, without much deliberation, some fanfare, and few tears, they jetted north for change of planes in New York and flight to Africa. Somewhere in their flight, Robert christened Red the Great American Big Game Hunter or simply Hunter.

By Robert's account, locals in Monrovia had fun with Red and told him big frightening tales of Gargantuan, deadly spiders and snakes and insects—sometimes in your bed. Little time for farewell or announcement, Red took first redeye, his flight in fright out of Africa. In less than a week after departing Birmingham, the Ex-Great American Big Game Hunter, or Ex-Hunter, as Robert called him, arrived back home to everyone's dismay—especially a stunned, shocked, and downright disillusioned wife Dolly-o.

Eighteen months later in late 1963, Robert returned home around Kennedy's assassination. In a matter of weeks, he took his old position and seniority on the Southern. In a few months, he became his union's Assistant Chairman of the Grievance Committee and within weeks he became General Chairman, a fulltime position. His days aboard engines ended at age 46. He handled and presented claims for enginemen all over the Southern and eventually other lines, companies, and travel occupations, even stewardesses. He negotiated with mediation, arbitration boards, Southern and union lawyers, and courts. He found his comfort zone and excelled. Gerry ran his office and knew most of his union friends and adversaries as well as he. They moved their office to atop Birmingham's 2121 building—vocation and view—relentless perspective.

Sometimes as things become what they should, when dreams and goals near fulfillment, and life goes your way as always wished, a closer inspection reveals cracks, seen and unseen fissures, hidden bumps and lumps and pits. Inflection points become obvious, undeniable, and irreversible. Invaluable perspective calls, a deadhead trip responds, and a downhill runaway train won't be back.

Gerry and Robert divorced in 1976. His freewheeling, rambling, constant travels, and endless work and life in Washington, DC, and her turning inward and away, devoured 35 years of marriage. He embraced DC, luxury world journeys, a German friend, new well-to-do circles. He found his freedom and dreams. She disdained rat race and morphed river rat. She became a loving heart and soul alone, taking up Tennessee River life, near Muscle Shoals, in a converted early 20th Century riverboat with waterfront view. She developed friends, kept family central, took in homeless dogs, and avoided looking back to hustle, bustle, and heartache of human condition.

Robert retired in 1986 at 67 with two impressive Birmingham parties, one at The Club with union people from all over and a next day bash at the Downtowner Club given by lawyer friends and associates. He had held his elected position for 22 years, a challenging task. People demand results and great things; they sour and defect. It's hard to be elected anything—even dog catcher—for 22 years.

Robert's Thanksgiving Wreck at Woodstock stood as Alabama's modern era's worst train wreck. In 1992, *The Sunset Limited* derailed into Mobile Bay and took dubious honor as worst. He and I watched newscasts of how in darkness and fog, a barge hit a bridge abutment, disrupted track alignment, and all those people dumped into night's black, deep, and muddy water. As before and from beginning, human error changes plans and lives—moves it all a little farther down main line.

More than anything military service remained his proudest moment, and he maintained a rapid pace for an aging, bearded gentleman some said looked more sea captain than fireman or engineer.

Asked how he was at any time, Not bad for a man my age and condition.

On New Year's Day, 1990, one of Gerry's adopted river mutts knocked her down, broke her hip. Living out her few weeks of temporary immobility, as prognosis foretold, at my request and urging, she recounted complete facts, details, and sidelights of her and Robert's life, as best she remembered. Judging her demeanor, she welcomed being pressed by me for information, and she enjoyed focusing on "The Thanksgiving Wreck at Woodstock", her viewpoint as she recalled it almost forty years after. I think it did her good to open and relive. She recited it all, and I took notes, though I don't know where they are.

A week into recovery a massive brain aneurysm killed her at home on January 20—age 66. She felt a few sharp sudden pains in her head over about 30 seconds as her veins bulged and retracted. In less than a minute she died at her kitchen table, in fact, eating fried baloney sandwich with mustard, lettuce, tomato, and onion. There must or should be some quote for that, but I don't know it and can't create it. Her ashes were spread, and a marker placed in Woodlawn, as she wished, next to Emma and Eugene, both dead since 1970. Her miniscule remains lie scattered a dozen miles from Willow Lane and nearby plots on a cemetery hill alongside the Alabama Great Southern mainline to Chattanooga, where Robert always fancied, in his poetic tongue in cheek fashion, she and he might eternize together—listening to whistles of old Train #17 and #18 rolling by.

Geraldine whispers, Poor Robert.

In early 1995, at 76, nagging dull pain and swelling issues in Robert's lower leg caused him to plan surgery to bypass, reverse, and graft an artery behind his knee in order to improve circulation. On completion, he and his female companion planned within a few months to fly to Hawaii for his marine division's reunion commemorating 50th anniversary of victory on Iwo Jima.

His post-surgery phone call caused me to fly next day Birmingham to DC. From there, a yellow cab ride, from his 14th and N apartment to George Washington Hospital, took only a few minutes. A cloudy, cold, good day for flu found me in a long black, wool ¾ length coat appearing more DC lawyer or FBI than forester and concerned son.

I walked down his long hall of globed lights to a background noise of echoed footsteps and squeaking hospital beds. Nurses moved around everywhere, taking care of business and uncomfortable patients, ignoring my arrival so early Sunday morning— before visiting time, breakfast still being served. In his room, he lay with eyes closed, motionless, and color fair all things considered.

I grasped his hand below his IV and held until his eyes opened. He looked much older than a few months before when he left Birmingham but always strong, proud, and determined.

"P." Papa.

He replied, eyes more open, "H." Hail.

I continued to hold on and stand beside his bed in silence listening again to a clatter of hospital sounds. I'm unsure how long I stood, uncertain of time—it didn't really matter looking back.

His eyes glossed over, all coming back after so long, They say I may never walk again.

We talked of small things in spurts—his female friend, his now cancelled trip to Diamond Head with marine buddies, of life in general. Things spun, can't imagine his feeling. His epidural went too deep, got his nerve. He woke from anesthesia, all feeling and movement gone from waist down. It will always be so.

It seemed as good a time as any, my brothers on their way, Sunday with sparse doctors and interruption, few people even knew where he was. Tell me everything, you talked so little. Tell me about growing up in Depression, having a part-time farmer and sheriff father. Tell me about Saipan and Iwo Jima.

And tell me about the Wreck. You seldom talked. Tell me.

At some point, thinking he dozed, I asked him or anyone listening above and beyond if he felt like Burns's disturbed mouse over 200 years before. He surprised me, opened his eyes, and stared into me without answer.

For almost five years, he struggled to move, lost body function, became imbalanced and gaunt. A man's man shriveled away, a victim of chance, human error, fortune, fate, and Divine will. For Robert in years of life, so many things went right against extreme, formidable circumstance and adversity, but it takes one mindless second to destroy him or anyone.

A few times in life, he called me lucky, without alluding to any one event or situation. I guess it was appropriate. Three hundred and fifty-three days after his Thanksgiving Wreck at Woodstock, I was born.

Work moved me from Alabama to Boise in late '90's. I traveled to Oakland in March 1999, for a week or two business trip. Conversations with brothers caused me to fly in haste to Birmingham and his home. He had been in bed for weeks and everyone, including hospice, considered him fading and bedridden until death. After his sons, me included, and his surviving brother Charles arrived, he rose up and came to his comfort chair on walker wearing his favorite tee—"Old Marines Never Die, They Just Go to Hell and Regroup". We conversed as if all rosy. He—head bloodied by chance and circumstance but unbowed—referred again to Henley, I am master of my fate, I am captain of my soul. He encased himself in quotes, purple robes of emperors, as he and his dear friend Wilder had foretold.

Later at night, we picked him up and placed him back in bed. He said, I know I'll never get up.

Robert died next day. A marine three-gun salute laid him to rest as makes him proudest. He lay on a hill northeast of Birmingham, near Gerry's and his "new home" of 1951, away from dim Willow Lane streetlight and beside the Alabama Great Southern Railroad mainline Birmingham to Chattanooga. And, as he told Gerry, now miles and years away, We can lie there and listen to Old 17 and 18 go by.

Unconquerable.

My 2007-08 "world" escape took me on rails in Brazil, England, Wales, Holland, Belgium, France, Spain, Austria, Italy, Switzerland, Germany, South Africa, Korea, Australia. One take away, considering obvious engineering, function, and timeliness of trains and otherwise, little wonder so often Germans whipped Europe and much of world at will.

A trip of such length and undertaking required a Canadian Transcontinental Railroad touch and, at last, a circular U. S. coast to coast finale.

In Utah, I was out between cars stretching and observing or gawking. Last thing a conductor does before departure is look up and down train, make sure everyone is on or off, all baggage and goods loaded or unloaded, everything detached or attached. On this day, the *Zephyr's* conductor completed her inspection by stepping on bottom step below my vestibule. She picked up her walkie-talkie and told engineer and fireman, Highball.

It hit me as peculiar how railroaders still repeat an antiquated term from 100 years before or more—especially females who, in large part, wouldn't have worked or been allowed to work railroad in those days.

Goodness, how things change—and my, how they don't.

The Zephyr took me east through Colorado highlands and spectacular Glenwood Canyon in White River National Forest. Every bit of my being looked forward to each anticipated mile— to a connection in Chicago and a ride south on *The City of New Orleans* through Mississippi darkness to sea. One last leg remained, *The Crescent* home through Woodstock. Faces and voices came to mind off and on—but accompanied me mile after mile—names like J. D. Pyler, engineer, at bottom of a pile of wreckage; Red Duncan swinging and dipping Gerry; Sam Pape, road foreman, who reacted perhaps too fast and jumped to his death; "The Wind", a local yokel who boasted in detail how he witnessed it all but refused an official statement; and, of course, Robert who saw it all in a flash. Everyone and everything changed in an instant, their plans, their future, their character. We maintained a gentle rock through Woodstock and curved north going home. At next crossing, our whistle blew a standard and familiar two longs, a short, and a long—Highball

Author

Richard Neil holds degrees from the University of Alabama and Auburn University. He has worked in the private sector and for the U. S. Air Force (Civilian), U. S. Forest Service, and U. S. Bureau of Land Management. He currently splits time between California and Alabama. *All the Livelong Day* is his second book.

richardneil.net
richardneilworks@gmail.com